More Praise for
Loving Someone Who Has Dementia

"With her work on ambiguous loss, Pauline Boss has shed much-needed light on a difficult human frontier. Now she brings her original insight to those caring for a loved one with dementia. Her knowledge is leavened by the rarer quality of wisdom. And so she truly offers a 'psychological journey toward meaning and hope' that practically addresses the hardest realities of life, love, self-care, and loss."

> —Krista Tippett, creator and host of public radio's
> *On Being*; author, *Einstein's God*

"The words in this book give caregivers a voice for what they feel and experience. They also give caregivers a 'place' to put their many emotions."

> —Peggye Dilworth-Anderson, PhD; professor,
> Department of Health Policy and Manage-
> ment, Gillings School of Global Public Health,
> University of North Carolina-Chapel Hill

"This is more than a survival guide for unpaid caregivers and support groups for families of those with dementia. It is an easily understood self-care manual for living well that illuminates options for finding balance and resilience while managing the ambiguous loss of having a loved one with dementia."

> —Macaran A. Baird, MD, MS; professor and
> head, University of Minnesota Medical School,
> Department of Family Medicine and Community
> Health

Loving Someone Who Has Dementia

*How to Find Hope While Coping
with Stress and Grief*

Pauline Boss, PhD

JOSSEY-BASS
A Wiley Imprint
www.josseybass.com

Published by Jossey-Bass
A Wiley Imprint
989 Market Street, San Francisco, CA 94103-1741—www.josseybass.com

Library of Congress Cataloging-in-Publication Data
Boss, Pauline.
  Loving someone who has dementia : how to find hope while coping with stress and grief / Pauline Boss.
    p. cm.
    Includes bibliographical references and index.
  ISBN 978-1-118-00229-2 (pbk.); ISBN 978-1-118-07725-2 (ebk.); ISBN 978-1-118-07726-9 (ebk.); ISBN 978-1-118-07728-3 (ebk.)
  1. Dementia—Patients—Care—Psychological aspects. 2. Dementia—Patients—Family relationships. 3. Grief. 4. Stress (Psychology) I. Title.
  RC521.B67 2011
  616.8′3—dc22

                                                                                    2011011957

Printed in the United States of America
FIRST EDITION
PB Printing 10 9 8 7 6 5 4 3 2 1

Dedicated to the many caregivers who inspired this book

and

to Elsbeth Elmer-Hammerli, who had dementia and whom I loved

Contents

Contents

Preface

I often thought about writing a book for families, but I was busy writing for academicians and professionals. As a retired professor, however, I have more options—and this message on my voice mail cinched it:

> I'm calling to make an appointment. Basically I just have one question to ask you. [long pause and then continuing with a weary and sad voice] How does a caretaker care for oneself ... when the work is soooo hard ... to care for the other ... [pause] I suppose that's the million-dollar question.

That caller convinced me that you all deserve an answer to this agonizing question. Yet many of you don't have the time or energy for therapy. I write this book then for the millions of you who now find yourselves asking the same question: "With the demands of caregiving, how can I possibly take care of myself?"

Researchers have found that caregiving can be dangerous to your health; it makes sense that in an aging society, caregiving becomes a public health issue. It's urgent that the rest of us help in any way we can to support you.

Toward this end, I write this book. It is not about how to give day-to-day-hands-on care; rather, it provides a new way to help you find meaning and hope in your relationship with someone you love who has dementia. The goal is to help you increase your resiliency—your ability to withstand and grow even stronger despite the stress and grief.

This book focuses specifically on a new lens or theory that can lessen the stress when a family member is here but not here. How did I get the idea for this new theoretical lens?

In the early 1970s, while studying family therapy with psychiatrist Carl Whitaker in my doctoral studies at the University of Wisconsin-Madison, I noticed that families with problem children often had psychologically absent fathers. They were *there but not there*, complaining (as fathers often did in the early seventies) that the child was the mother's business, not his, and didn't we know that he had to get back to work? Whitaker, of course, did not agree. Nor did I.

Relatively quickly, I came to see that any family member, not just a father, could be psychologically absent while physically present. In a sociology seminar, also at the University of Wisconsin-Madison, I began to develop the theory of ambiguous loss, and it became the topic of my doctoral dissertation in 1975, which focused on families of pilots missing in action after the Vietnam War. This was ambiguous loss of the *physical* type.

In the 1980s, now a professor at the University of Minnesota, I tested the theory of ambiguous loss again, this time with family caregivers whose loved ones had Alzheimer's disease. This was ambiguous loss of the *psychological* type. Ever since, in research and clinical work I've studied the effects on relationships when one person is psychologically absent—when a person you love is physically here, but gone psychologically.

Along with teaching, research, and clinical work, I have trained professionals who work with the psychological losses of dementia as well as those who work with families of the physically missing (in New York after 9/11, in Kosovo, in the Gulf Coast after Katrina, and in Miami after the Haitian earthquake). All continue to provide ideas that broaden guidelines to be more culturally inclusive. My training of professionals continues today.

The research today is conducted primarily by a second generation of scholars, some of whom studied with me at the University of Minnesota, but many from around the world are now testing the theory of ambiguous loss in other cultures.[1] I couldn't be happier about this.

In 2009, at the beginning of winter, I began writing this book, motivated by my long-standing belief that if people can understand a problem, they are better able to cope with it. The theory of ambiguous loss is grounded in that premise.

A year has passed, and snow is falling again. It's a welcome quiet in the midst of what are stressful times for the millions of people who are now caring for a loved one who has dementia. May this book and the ideas within it prove useful to you in your search for meaning and hope.

Pauline Boss
Saint Paul, Minnesota
December 2010

Acknowledgments

I am deeply grateful to the thousands of individuals, couples, and families who have shared their stories with me in either therapy or research. It is from you that I have learned about resiliency and how it can be found in the midst of ambiguity and adversity. Specifically, I thank the many caregivers of people with dementia with whom I have worked. It was you who inspired me to write this book.

* Thanks to the Wayne Caron Family Caregiving Center support group at the University of Minnesota and to Tim Harper for providing feedback on my original book proposal.
* Thanks to my agent, James Levine, who guided me in the transition from academia to writing for the general public.
* Thanks to Alan Rinzler, Nana Twumasi, and Marjorie McAneny of Jossey-Bass/Wiley for being so enthusiastic about this book, and for Nana's skillful and patient editing. Thanks also to Carol Hartland, production

editor, and Michele Jones, copyeditor, for their special skills.

✻ Thanks to the professionals and caregivers who read earlier versions of the manuscript and gave valuable feedback: Barbara Sidders, Dorothea Torstenson, Rebecca Sullivan, Ann Sheffels, Lorraine Beaulieu, Diane Papalia, Carey Sherman, Mona Fraki, Connie Steele, Carol Riggs, Elaine Morgan, and Dudley Riggs. Thanks also to Kate Mulligan for her feedback.

✻ Thanks to my longtime assistant, Carol Mulligan, without whom I could not do this work. Her technical skills and penchant for detail make all of my books, and especially this one, possible.

✻ Finally, thanks to my dear husband, children, and grandchildren. Their constant support and love carry me through the inherent loneliness of writing.

Introduction

Here's the problem: as of 2011, there were 5.4 million Americans living with Alzheimer's disease.[1] The number increases if the other diseases and conditions that cause irreversible dementia are included. Every sixty-nine seconds, someone in America today develops Alzheimer's disease.[2] By 2050, the rate will increase to every thirty-three seconds.[3] Said another way, few families now—and fewer yet in the future—will be untouched by Alzheimer's or other dementias.

More women than men are susceptible to dementia, primarily because they tend to live longer.[4] In addition, race, ethnicity, education, and location also influence the prevalence of dementias.[5] One fact, however, is consistent: any increase in dementia leads to an increased need for caregivers. What do researchers tell us about them?

As of 2010, there were 14.9 million unpaid caregivers in the United States.[6] Not surprisingly, 60 percent are female—wives, daughters, daughters-in-law, granddaughters, and friends.[7] More surprising, the typical caregiver is relatively young. According to a 2011 report of the Alzheimer's Association, 67 percent of caregivers are between the ages of thirty-five and sixty-four. On either side of this largest group, caregivers range from very young (10 percent under the age of thirty-five) to very old (23 percent sixty-five or older).[8] Wives and daughters do most of the caregiving for persons with dementia; they also report the most negative effects on their own well-being.[9]

Many caregivers find themselves in what is called the sandwich generation, simultaneously caring for young children and elderly parents. Tending both to younger and older generations—and perhaps also to a marriage—such caregivers find themselves pulled from all sides, squeezed for time, and struggling with divided loyalties—a recipe for high anxiety and extreme stress.

■ ■

If someone you love has dementia, this book represents a psychological journey toward meaning and hope. We begin with ideas to help you understand why dementia can be so confusing and stressful, then follow with guidelines to help you cope and stay resilient. Throughout, my message to you is that participating in a less than perfect relationship can deepen your humanity.

My primary focus is on how to find meaning in dementia's unique kind of loss—what I call *ambiguous loss*. Dementia is a prime example of ambiguous (unclear) loss;

making sense of it is especially difficult because a loved one is simultaneously here and gone. It's as though there's a stranger in the house; the relationship you once had is thus deeply altered. Without clarity or clear finality, you're held in limbo, blocked from grieving and making sense of it all. Because of the incongruence between absence and presence, ambiguous loss is the most stressful kind of loss. Clients tell me that even a death in the family would be less painful. There is certainty in death, and thus more opportunity for finding meaning in it.

Who Is This Book For?

This book is meant for anyone who cares for—or cares about—a person who has some kind of dementia. It's for you if you're doing hands-on or long-distance caregiving. It's for you if you are experiencing sadness and anxiety due to caring about someone with dementia. It is also for others—friends, relatives, clergy, medical professionals—who want a resource that discusses the complexities of a caregiver's loss and what to do about it.

In an aging society, we are *all* vulnerable to the need either to give care—or to receive it. It's not an isolated problem. Until there is a cure, dementia, regardless of its source, remains a twenty-first-century epidemic—and we are all in it together.

With only a few degrees of separation, we now all know someone who has dementia or who is caregiving.

Yet even when it's close by, many people turn their heads and don't notice the frequency of what's happening. Until we all pay more attention, until we see caring as important, we are marginalizing and isolating the family caregivers who contribute so much to keeping dementia patients at home for as long as possible.

Until recently, families have tended to designate one family member (thus the term "primary" caregiver) to do the work of caregiving while the rest of the family and community carried on with their lives. They likely breathed a sigh of relief when they didn't have to put in what is called the "thirty-six-hour day."[10] But now it's time for all of us to acknowledge, appreciate, and directly help caregivers—the one down the street, the one in your congregation, the one in your family—because simply put, it takes a village. One person can't do it alone and stay healthy.

What often endangers the emotional and physical health of caregivers is their isolation. Unlike dementia, this problem can be fixed. We can do better. We can try harder to understand the caregiving experience. And that is what this book is for.

Caregivers are a devoted army of family and friends who provide most of the dementia care and who work for no pay and no benefits. They save our government (and taxpayers) millions of dollars by reducing the time dementia patients spend in institutional care settings. Surely we can pay closer attention to their contributions.

Policymakers, community leaders, neighbors, friends, and relatives need to acknowledge their work—and lend a hand so that caregivers can stay more socially connected. After all, human connection is what keeps us healthy.

What I Mean by "Dementia"

Dementia, whether from illness or injury, is a condition of the brain that leads to the loss of remembering, thinking, reasoning, and judgment. Gradually, even the simplest tasks of daily living—dressing, feeding, and toileting—require help. Dementia itself is not a disease, but rather a group of symptoms that results from other diseases or conditions. The most common is Alzheimer's disease, a fatal disease that accounts for over half of all cases of dementia.[11] Dementia changes one's personality, mood, and behavior, so existing relationships are strained. Thus dementia is more than a physiological condition. It is a *relational* condition that deeply affects those who care *for* and care *about* the patient.

What is relevant to the thesis of this book is the factor of incurability, which creates the deepest and longest-lasting ambiguity and stress for caregivers. Approximately fifty causes of dementia exist now, some treatable, some not. In this book, I limit my discussion to those that are as yet *not* curable—Alzheimer's disease, vascular dementia (tiny strokes), Lewy body dementia, frontal lobe dementia, Huntington's disease, Parkinson's disease, AIDS dementia complex, and Creutzfeldt-Jakob disease (what is also called mad cow disease), among others.[12]

The lack of resolution is what makes the case of dementia so compelling in the study of human resiliency. How do people live with a loved one who is gone psychologically but still here physically? In the absence of a cure—or the finality of death—how do people live in this shadow land? These are the questions that I will try to answer in subsequent chapters.

Before we proceed, I need to add a note about traumatic brain injury, which can also lead to dementia. After much thought, I have decided not to address the ambiguous loss of traumatic brain injury in this book, even though it is the signature wound from our wars in the Middle East. Why? Because progressive dementia is not always the outcome of traumatic brain injury, and because younger patients and their spouses or parents differ from older patients and their families in their dynamics and developmental life stages. Having worked with the families of these young people wounded in Iraq and Afghanistan, I see them very differently. They are not families in the last half of life, but young families trying to build a life together despite terrible wounds in both body and mind. Although there are commonalities, their story deserves a book of its own.

Why I'm Writing This Book

Although dementia at any stage is a difficult experience for anyone, it is especially stressful for those of us who like to be in charge of our own destinies. Accustomed to being in control, we feel helpless about dementia. Yet there is a way to feel better. When we can't control the dementia, we can still control how we perceive and manage the situation. And therein lies a caregiver's window for hope.

Although I'm not technically a boomer, I relate to their generation of can-do people accustomed to finding solutions to problems. As a Swiss American Protestant professor who was socialized to believe that I could solve anything if I worked hard enough, I too have struggled with feelings of helplessness, as I watched dear ones slip away with illnesses that had no cure—my grandmother's dementia, my little brother's polio, and my sister's cancer. Today, polio is prevented and cancer has better treatments, but we still face problems that have no solution, and dementia remains one of them. There are many ways to feel less helpless with this kind of loss, and I will share them with you. Instead of offering a how-to caregiving book (there are already many good ones), I've developed a new lens through which to make sense of your situation so that you can manage it—and thereby feel stronger for this journey with dementia.

How to Read This Book

This book is designed to be read alone or with a group. It is your guide for self-reflection as well as discussion with others. Each chapter can stand alone and has its own topic. Read it in any way you wish. Although related themes run throughout the book, you may, if you are busy or exhausted, want to focus on only one chapter at a time. I hope you find the information useful and calming for what is likely to be a long and painful journey.

Know that I do not discuss the illnesses and conditions that cause dementia, nor do I discuss the medical technicalities of dementia. Rather, I focus on the challenges you face *relationally* when someone you love has dementia.

Here is a brief summary of the chapters, so that you can best decide which area to focus on as you read:

Chapter One, "The Ambiguous Loss of Dementia," explains what ambiguous loss is, how it relates to you, and why it can cause depression and anxiety.

Chapter Two, "The Complications of Both Loss and Grief," makes the case that unresolved loss causes unresolved grief. What this means for you is that your complicated grief is to be expected. It is not your fault. The complicated grief is caused by ambiguous loss—in this case, by the dementia, which requires a special kind of grieving.

Chapter Three, "Stress, Coping, and Resiliency," helps you identify your own stress issues more specifically.

Once you have done this, your coping can begin. Knowing what the problem is allows you to deal with it. How caregivers do this will differ depending on their beliefs and values.

Chapter Four, "The Myth of Closure," tells you why closure is the wrong goal with dementia, and what you can learn from the many people who live comfortably without it. Many caregivers embrace the ambiguity rather than fight it; they offer much you can learn from about living with ambiguity and uncertainty.

Chapter Five, "The Psychological Family," introduces the idea that you may have, in addition to your biological family, a family in your heart and mind, and that this psychological family can be very comforting when you feel alone and isolated, or overwhelmed.

Chapter Six, "Family Rituals, Celebrations, and Gatherings," focuses on ways to help you stay connected to others while you are providing care. Human connection is essential to your well-being, and rituals are a way to make such connections regularly.

Chapter Seven, "Seven Guidelines for the Journey," is the core of the book. It provides guidelines for finding your way on your long and arduous journey with dementia. I intentionally use the term *guidelines* rather than *tips* or *rules*, because I want these ideas to be useful to a broader diversity of families and caregivers who have varying beliefs and values.

Chapter Eight, "Delicious Ambiguity," presents the positive side of dementia's ambiguity. Without romanticizing the pain, seeing the good side gives you back some sense of control and takes away some of the terror.

Chapter Nine, "The Good-Enough Relationship," suggests that a "good-enough" relationship can be good. In fact, most of us already have had such relationships, because loved ones are rarely fully present both physically and psychologically. That experience can help you now as you experience your more extreme situation with dementia.

Although each chapter contains separate ideas, there is overlap so that you can review or read one chapter at a time. The common theme throughout is that you can find meaning in your changed relationship. Once you make sense of it, you can more easily discover new hope and peace despite the stress of dementia's ambiguous loss.

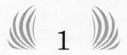

The Ambiguous Loss of Dementia

How Absence and Presence Coexist

The test of a first-rate intelligence is the ability to hold two opposed ideas in the mind at the same time, and still retain the ability to function.

—F. SCOTT FITZGERALD, THE CRACK-UP, 1945, p. 69

Rarely in human relationships are people completely absent or present. For this reason, loss and ambiguity are core elements in the human experience. With dementia, however, they merge into what I call *ambiguous loss*.[1]

Ambiguous loss is a loss that is unclear; it has no resolution, no closure. This unique and devastating kind of loss can be physical or psychological, but in either case, a family member's status as absent or present remains hazy.

Dementia creates ambiguous loss. The duality of your loved one's being absent and present at the same time is confusing, and finding meaning (or making sense of your situation) becomes immensely challenging. Without meaning, it's hard to cope. It's hard to manage even your day-to-day responsibilities. Ambiguous loss ruptures your relationship as you knew it. What you had before your loved one's dementia set in, and the way you were together, are now gone.

With dementia, something is definitely lost; you feel it, but no one comes to you—as they do after a loved one dies—to validate or support your loss. People even say things like "You're lucky; you still have your mate" or "You still have your parent." But you know you don't, really.

Health care professionals might distance themselves from you because you're not the patient, just the caregiver. Making you feel even more confused and alone, none of the usual customs and rituals used to manage grief fit your kind of loss. You are on your own in a limbo that all too often goes unnoticed (or denied) by the larger community. Perhaps it is simply convenient for society to let unpaid family caregivers deal with dementia patients on their own. Or perhaps it's too troubling for others to see what they cannot fix. For many reasons, it takes extraordinary strength to be a caregiver.

Gone, Not Gone

In my therapy practice, I worked with Jenny, who told me her husband was "slowly slipping away into another world." She knew the diagnosis, dementia due to Alzheimer's, and realized that the journey would be long—years, maybe decades. But she was desperate to find some relief from her anger and confusion. She wanted her husband back; he'd been a successful businessman, a loving husband and father—but he was no longer the man she knew. Gone—but still there.

The event that made Jenny reach out for help came when her husband of forty years became short tempered. He no longer treated her kindly. She said she felt as though there was a stranger in the house. This was not the relationship she wanted. She felt betrayed and abandoned.

Such uncanny transformation brings shifts not only in relationships but also in the way we see ourselves. Consider these difficult questions:

Am I still married if my spouse doesn't know me anymore?
Is he still a parent to our children if he doesn't know them
anymore?
Am I still the daughter if I am now mothering my mother,
my father?

People vary in how they answer such questions, but they all struggle with them. Jenny felt as if she were alone now and thus obliged to rethink who she was. With deep sadness, she said, "I feel like I'm leaving the shore for an unknown place."

Jenny was experiencing the loss of her husband's mind and memory—and also their relationship as it had been prior to his Alzheimer's diagnosis. He was with her physically, but virtually absent psychologically. This incongruence was confusing and painful.

I told her that what she was experiencing was ambiguous loss—the most difficult kind of loss because there is *no possibility of closure*.

Having a name for the problem, she could begin her coping process. We talked about possible choices. She might choose to act as if nothing were wrong or, going to the other extreme, as if he were already gone and out of her life. She said she had tried the former and couldn't do the latter. I suggested she consider the middle ground.

"What is that?" she asked.

"You can learn how to live with the ambiguity that comes with dementia."

Although living with ambiguity is not an easy task in a culture that values certainty, Jenny chose to wrestle with not knowing what was coming next or how it would end. But now she understood that the culprit was neither her husband nor herself, but the illness. Dementia brings with it something mysterious that skews a relationship beyond human expectation. Knowing that it was not her fault, she was better able to begin coping—*not* to find a solution to the problem but rather to live with the lack of solution and the unanswered questions.

Loving Half a Person

In my therapy practice, I see many people like Jenny—women and men who come to me because they are at their wits' end trying to figure out what is happening to them and their relationship with someone they love. It is not just about the exhausting and lonely caregiving role, but also about how to make sense of the situation they now find themselves in—without losing who they are in the process.

Regardless of its cause, dementia's ambiguous loss can debilitate even the healthiest of us. This is the struggle: making sense out of a nonsensical situation. You come to realize that life now is dramatically altered. Your loss is great, but there is no sympathy card; no one sits Shiva or holds a wake. Instead, there is a lonely and oft-misunderstood mourning—a chronic sadness[2]—with an indefinite beginning and indefinite end.

A New York psychologist who was also a caregiver, Carolyn Feigelson, asks a painful question: "How is it possible to lose half a person? Half is dead, half remains alive.... Unlike a fairy tale whose premise is poetic reality in which nothing can surprise the reader, the uncanny story violates the observer's trust in reality."[3] To be sure, caregivers who live with ambiguous loss live with a reality that is broken and no longer trustworthy. Their loss is irrational, illogical, and absurd, and yet real.

Whether dementia stems from illness or injury, the challenge is to embrace the ambiguity and confusion. This doesn't mean passively submitting—or settling. Rather, it means discovering your choices and making decisions about how to find some continuity in the midst of chaos and change. It means trying to find some clarity in the midst of ambiguity. And live with ambiguity we must, if not earlier in life, then certainly as we grow older.

Even in normal times, we are most often apart from those we love. I go to work in one place, my husband in another, and our children in yet another. Some are in other states, thousands of miles away. Friends are scattered around the globe. In this mobile society, most of us are separated from those we love most of the time. But contemporary families seem to take what dissonance there is between physical and psychological presence in stride. Is this because we know that we can come together again whenever we wish? Unlike with dementia, such loss is retrievable. We can fix the loss with an airplane ticket or phone call. (There are, of course, obstacles that prevent reunions, such as cost, war, or political strife.)

Once we see how rare it is for couples and families to be fully present for one another, physically and psychologically, we realize that most of us already possess some skills for living with the ambiguity of separation and distance—and surviving it. This previous experience, albeit different, helps teach us how to survive loving someone with dementia.

6

Finding the Middle Ground

With dementia, absence and presence coexist. Struggling too hard for clarity can lead to false answers that are attempts to erase the ambiguity. What I see most often is either premature closure (she is already dead to me, so I don't visit her anymore) or a denial that anything has been lost (he is just naturally forgetful, so he can still drive). Unless we consciously work hard to think about embracing ambiguity, any of us could quite easily fall into absolute thinking. This does not work with ambiguous loss and the real complexity you face.

When someone you love has dementia, the task is to increase your tolerance for the stress of ambiguity. To begin doing this, work at learning how to hold two opposing views at the same time—my parent is here, and not here; my mate is no longer the person I married, but still someone I love and will care for. Don't give up on loved ones when they are no longer able to be who they were.

Paraphrasing F. Scott Fitzgerald, learning to hold two opposing ideas in your mind at the same time allows you to move to the middle ground instead of sticking with the extremes. In the case of dementia, rather than the unfortunate extremes of either denial or acting as if the person were already dead and gone, there is a better choice: see absence and presence as coexisting. This is the best way to survive ambiguous loss.

With more paradoxical thinking, we live with the tension of conflicting ideas about absence and presence. Someone we love is both here and gone. When there's no cure to an illness or condition, the only window for hope is to become more comfortable with ambiguity and a less than perfect relationship.

Thinking in a more open way requires us to focus on the meaning of our relationship with an ill person rather than on what is normal. Gradually, as we accept the ambiguity, we can make sense of even an ambiguous loss, and thus more easily cope with it.

Adjusting Goals

Ultimately, the goal is not to end your relationship but to achieve a psychological shift or transformation in your thinking that fits a relationship which is now drastically changed by dementia. The goal is to accept the ambiguity.

When to Say Good-Bye

I continued to see Jenny when she had time. As I typically do with the caregivers I work with, I encouraged her to say good-bye to her husband at some point, even before death. She would know when that time came. Jenny kept a journal, and shares parts of it to help us understand how difficult the process really is:

8

January, after diagnosis

This is such a lonely disease. I am surrounded by people, but so lonely. The loneliness comes from being with someone who is no longer able to reach back to me. Loneliness is a different emotion than solitude. I have always enjoyed moments of solitude in life ... but the loneliness is deafening. There is such an "empty space" in my life now. Sometimes I look at John while he is sleeping, trying to remember what our life was like.

July, two years later

My son called today. I am so thankful for his weekly calls from another state. It has been a great gift to me because he is not afraid to give me insight to help me keep perspective. Today I told him I am fighting for a quality of life for John ... and he gave me a reality check in his answer. He said, "The fact is, Mom, Dad's quality of life is not going to get better, he will progressively deteriorate ... and your hoping he will get better is keeping you from fighting for a quality of life for yourself." He continued, "You need to realize that the man you have been married to for 40 years is now gone, and it may even feel that you are married to a stranger, one that you don't even like."

After that conversation, I took a drive to clear my head. I popped in a CD by Josh Groban that my granddaughter had left in my car. It was new to me. The song, "You're Still You," came on and the words stunned me—especially the ones about "through the darkness I still see your light." I realized that I still hold the memories of our years together, so I could see that light of him in the midst of the darkness, but no longer could he see my light since his memories were not only diminishing, but also leaving altogether. I pulled off to the side of the turnpike and listened to that song again and again, letting the tears flow down my face in convulsing sobs. I realized the time had come to say "good-bye" to the man who was, and say "hello" to the man who now is. That became a turning point. I let the tears of grief flow freely and let myself really feel the loss of my best friend, confidant, and biggest cheerleader in life.

April, three years later (after her husband was placed in a nursing home)
Today I went to see John as usual and take him for our daily walk. Today we walk inside the facility because it is still too cold for an outside jaunt. Fran (not her real name), another patient, came to me and wanted to walk with us. She calls John her boyfriend, and they have developed somewhat of an attachment. "Sure, walk with us, Fran," I answer. There we were, walking down the halls of the facility, she on one side and I on the other side of John, holding hands. The two of them carry on a disjointed conversation, and I can tell that somehow through it they connect to one another. It may sound strange, but I was glad

for their friendship with each other. I am glad that they both receive some pleasure through their interaction. She tells me, "This is my boyfriend." And I answer, "Well, he certainly is a good one." She pats his hand and he smiles.

As I get ready to leave, I hug John and he says to me, "It's so nice to meet you." I knew this day would come, but somehow I am not ready for it. The tears course down my face. The last tie of recognition he had is gone. I walk with him every day, but I am alone now in knowing about our precious life together over these many years. I grieve.

June

Today when I arrived, John was lying down and I could tell he was thinking about something. He suddenly showed a moment of lucidity when I asked him, "What are you thinking?" Most of the time I can't understand what he is saying, but he said, "I'm scared." When I asked him what scared him, I couldn't understand his answer, so I asked, "About the future?" He said, "Yes." I was overwhelmed with compassion for him, knowing that somewhere inside of him he is still feeling and has no way of expressing the thoughts. I hugged him, assuring him that I was scared, too, but that we would walk each day together. I assured him about how much I loved him, how much his family and friends love him, and we all wish he weren't having to go through this. And as

11

quickly as it came, that moment of awareness
was gone.

John is deteriorating quite rapidly now. I can't
imagine a world without him in my life. The
essence of who he is has been gone for a long time
now. And he is changing almost daily. His long
journey is almost over. And I grieve each change.
And I say another good-bye.

Jenny's poignant story tells us that saying good-bye to
someone who has dementia is not a one-time event. You
do it over and over again each time you see a new loss.
But doing so helps bring about a more peaceful parting
for both.

Balancing Individuality and Togetherness

When one person in a couple is healthier than the other
(not an unusual circumstance in families today), the
marital or parental relationship becomes skewed, with the
healthier person making most of the decisions and the ill
person primarily on the receiving end. But herein lies the
caregiver's conundrum. You need both individuality and
togetherness.[4]

Indeed, there are many caregivers who say they
receive as much benefit from taking care of their partner
or parent as they give, but they also report being isolated,
overworked, lacking in sleep, and unable to attend to their

own needs. Although we hope there is mutual benefit for both patient and caregiver, the startling statistic from researchers is this: caregivers die at a rate 63 percent higher than people the same age who are not caring for someone with dementia.[5]

What this means is that caregiving is dangerous to your health. This is all the more reason for professionals and the larger community to work more patiently with the persons who give the care and now bear the burden of their loved ones' survival. They deserve empathy and respect. For the sake of their health, they need community and professional support to maintain a separate identity along with the role of caregiver.

Thinking Both-And (not Either-Or)

When someone is both here and gone, the way to lower your stress is with *both-and thinking*—that is, understanding that two contradictory ideas can both be true. This is the reality of dementia.

Paradoxical thinking can help you see ambiguity as a natural, even spiritual, condition. Living with dementia, even from a secular perspective, requires a trust in the unknown that things will work out, and that whatever happens can be managed. If you're still hanging in there, it means you have already expanded your tolerance for ambiguity. I congratulate you. That resiliency is needed to carry you through on this journey of dementia.

Changing Perceptions

Living well usually means having access to information that enables you to make choices and decisions about how to think, feel, and act. Most of us prefer to stay in charge and avoid what has no answer. However, when there is a lack of clear information, as is the case with an ambiguous loss, we think and feel on the basis of our perceptions. We go with what we *think* we see. To live well in the absence of clear information, know that your perceptions are pliable; you can change them to lower your stress. Try a new way of thinking to avoid the stress of unrealistic absolutes. With dualistic both-and thinking, you may find you can shift your perceptions more easily.

To lower your stress, use both-and thinking to change perceptions:

- She is both gone and still here.
- I take care of both him and myself.
- I am both a caregiver and a person with my own needs.
- I both wish it was over and wish that my loved one keeps on living.
- I am both sad about my lost hopes and dreams and happy about some new hopes and dreams.

I thought of shifting perceptions while standing in the Louvre a few years ago looking at the Mona Lisa. Is she smiling or not? The answer depends on my perception—and *that*, fortunately, can change. We can see in ambiguity what we want. And therein lies the hope for Jenny and all of you who live with dementia.

When you are living with an illness or condition that has (as yet) no cure, hope lies in your perception and ability to change. This is creative adaptation. Seeing yourself and your situation in a new light can open doors. You begin to meet new people while also sticking by your loved one. You expand who you are beyond the role of caregiver by making new connections either in person or virtually on the Internet. Or you see ambiguity suddenly in more normal, even fun activities—playing cards, gaming, fishing—and you become less stressed by it. Your perception of ambiguity as terror is changing.

It is not easy to let go of the need for certainty, but in the mysteries of ambiguous relationships, there is also an opportunity to grow stronger. Hope lies in understanding that you are doing the best you can.

To be sure, most of us don't like to "settle." We won't go down without a fight. Good. Let's find a cure for illnesses and conditions that cause dementia. Let's find help for caregivers so that their health is not compromised. But in the end, regardless of how hard we work or fight, we can't win this game. Death is part of the circle of life, with or without dementia.

15

What we can do is live each day well, with more tranquility and peacefulness, recognizing that things will not always go our way. Bad things can indeed happen to good, smart, hardworking people.

We must, of course, fight for what is reasonable, but we must also choose sometimes to let go. To do this means balancing control with acceptance. It means embracing the ambiguity when a loss has no closure. We live lives of curiosity instead of lives focused on expectations.

What is around the next corner? We don't really know, do we? Like exploring the mountains or riding the rapids down the Colorado River, it's another adventure.

■ ■

When Jenny's husband came back home for his last months, he required around-the-clock care, and her tasks became extremely difficult. I was concerned that she was losing herself in the work. But eventually this changed. As she realized she couldn't control everything, she began to see the situation differently:

> There is still the element of control that is not only unhealthy for me, but for the poor people around me. So I have fired myself from being my world's organizer. I think I monitor the environment in order to keep everyone happy and away from conflict ... not good. So I am working

on making peace with the idea of conflict being
healthy sometimes. I realize that I make decisions
based on "Will someone be upset if I do this?"
and allow the "What if they get upset?" to cheat
me from some healthy decisions for myself which
will give my life meaning and purpose.

And then Jenny suddenly shifts, balancing her story of
loss with one of new hope:

I am going to the University tomorrow to make
arrangements for the "interests test" and to start
the process of application. I don't know what the
future holds, but getting ready for fall classes will
be good, even if something happens to delay
this goal.

Jenny never made it to classes that fall. Her husband
died, and after the funeral, there were months of details
that needed her attention. Then she found out she was
ill, got the necessary treatment, and also packed up and
moved to a smaller house in an area she loved. Now, a
few years later, Jenny is thriving. She is settled in her new
home, energetic as usual, and surrounded by good friends
and activities, with children and grandchildren not too
far away. She has not forgotten what she calls "walking
through the heartbreak of dementia," but she is also moving forward with her life in a new way.

The ability of people to grow stronger despite loss continues to amaze and teach me. Human beings are naturally resilient—if others don't stand in their way with judgment and stigma. Each person, each couple, and each family finds ways of transforming despair to hope, but overall, at the core of this process is increasing their tolerance for ambiguity. Even if they don't know what the future holds, they're willing to try something new. To do this, it helps to have more information. One has to know what the problem really is. People continue to tell me that it helps to have a name for what they are experiencing. Knowing what the problem is and that it's not their fault, they can more easily cope with a new and difficult situation.

Ambiguous loss is a unique kind of loss that not only challenges coping but also seriously complicates the grieving process. I will explain further in the next chapter.

⚜ *Ideas for Reflection and Discussion* ⚜

❋ Most of you already possess some skills for living with the ambiguity of separation and distance—and knowing how to survive it.

❋ Before you can manage the stress that comes with caring for someone with dementia, you must know what the problem is. Label it.

18

�֍ The culprit causing distress is not the person who has dementia, nor is it you. It's the ambiguity that surrounds your loss.

�֍ When someone you love is here, then gone, then here again, then gone again, his or her presence has two meanings. Not knowing which of the two is real, you may feel distressed and anxious. Try accepting both perceptions as true.

�֍ Promote both-and (not either-or) thinking.

   �֍ Because there's no perfect solution and no absolute answer to whether your loved one is here or gone, you need to be able to think both-and—dualistically. It is helpful, therefore, to practice. For example, see your loved one as *both* here *and* gone; see yourself as doing *both* caregiving *and* connecting to other people. Create some more both-and lines to fit your situation.

   ✷ Although some stress will remain, balancing two different ideas in your mind at the same time is less stressful than continuing to search for an absolute solution.

The Complications of Both Loss and Grief

[About his deceased daughter, Freud said,] "She is here," and he showed me a tiny locket that he wore, fastened to his watch-chain.

—HILDA DOOLITTLE, QUOTED IN PETER GAY, FREUD: A LIFE FOR OUR TIME, 2006, p. 392

Researchers tell us that the main cause of distress for caregivers like Jenny is neither the burden of caregiving nor the severity of illness, but rather the stress caused by not being able to resolve the problem—not being able to ease their loved one's suffering, not having control over their own lives anymore, not knowing what roles to play, not knowing when it will end, and not knowing whether they are doing a good job, considering that there's often no positive feedback from the patient, extended family, or larger community. The caregiver is alone.

Complicated Loss, Complicated Grief

To understand the effects of dementia's ambiguous loss and how to cope, it helps to know about complicated grief and complicated loss. Many of you caregivers, like Jenny, are experiencing both.

Complicated grief is grief that goes on too long. The grieving person doesn't follow what psychiatrists call the normal path of grieving, with symptoms of sadness, poor appetite, insomnia coming to an end after two to six months. In such cases, the person is diagnosed with having a major depressive episode.[1] It is no longer normal grieving and implies personal pathology.

In the case of dementia, however, the type of loss is the problem, not the mental and emotional state of the caregiver. Dementia creates a loss that is ongoing; thus your grief is also ongoing. Your grieving may not be over for years, even decades. With ambiguous loss, this is normal.

Ambiguous loss—in this case, dementia—causes complicated loss. As many caregivers say, "Oh, it's the situation that's crazy, not me." Although that is not quite how I would put it, they are right. Rather than telling them they have "complicated grief," I say that their chronic sadness and mixed emotions more accurately result from "a pattern of impaired interaction."[2] It's a relational problem due to some external condition (in this case dementia) that's outside your control, and it's not your fault. There can be no closure because the dementia continues to test your acceptance of loss.

One caregiver summed it up succinctly:

> The occasional flashes of lucidity can be treasured moments ... invitations to connect that offer surprise and delight. But at the same time, they call into question the course of care. Has the absent affect of the person with memory loss been a function of the disease—or incorrect medications? The fragile acceptance of loss is retested over and over again.

This roller coaster of losing, finding, and losing again will erode anyone's stability and strength. Feelings of helplessness lead to depression and anxiety. Of course, symptoms need to be treated, but attributing them to the caregiver's psychic weakness is neither valid nor fair. For this reason, the complicated grief that accompanies the ambiguous loss of dementia should be in a diagnostic category of its own.

Living with someone both here and gone is a bizarre experience that can produce terrible pain and anxiety. To ease the stress, it helps to understand the differences between death and ambiguous loss, and why one is more likely to lead to what has been called normal grief and the other to complicated grief.

What's the Difference Between Normal Grief and Complicated Grief?

Consider Mary and Ruth: Mary's husband died following a massive stroke while mowing the lawn. The ambulance came, a doctor pronounced him dead, a pastor came to say prayers, and a few days after there was a wake and a funeral. People sent flowers, gave eulogies, read scripture, recited poetry, sang songs, and shared food and stories. All of this provided Mary with solace—plus the certainty that her husband was really gone. That his loss was irretrievable was clear, acknowledged officially and by the community at large. She was sad and still numb from the shock, but her family and friends were there to help her grieve and find some meaning in her loss. There were familiar rituals to help her honor and mourn her husband—and most important, she was not left alone in her grief. Her community was there for her.

Ruth's husband also had a massive stroke, but he survived, albeit with cognitive loss. As years passed by, he slipped deeper into dementia. Ruth continued to care for him, but felt a deep and chronic sadness as if there had been a death—but then felt guilty because her husband was still alive. She experienced mixed emotions and doubt about how to feel, who to be, and what, if anything, remained of their relationship. She felt alone. Few outsiders noticed all that she had lost or that she was constantly in mourning. This included well-meaning professionals and relatives, who were often relieved not to be responsible for caring for someone who was taking a long time to die.

Which woman was experiencing the more complicated loss and was thus more likely to suffer from complicated grief? Ruth's loss was complicated by ambiguity and the confusion of not knowing when her loss would be final. Mary's loss was, of course, very painful as well, but she had the benefit of informational clarity. She was less haunted by doubt. She was therefore freer to move forward with her life as a widow. Ruth, in contrast, was stuck in a limbo that had no immediate resolution.

Because different kinds of loss require different kinds of grieving, knowing which kind you are experiencing helps you understand and thus cope. For Mary, grieving began as normally expected—*after* the death of a loved one. For Ruth, it began *before* death.

Although grieving the loss of someone who is still alive is understandable, it is in itself a complication that will confuse you. Regardless of the dementia's source, your having to accept the loss and acknowledge the need to grieve while someone is still alive defies logic. It is counterintuitive. Yet Ruth's kind of complicated loss—with its high probability of complicated grief—is surprisingly common.

Complex Grieving for Ambiguous Loss

The basic premise of ambiguous loss theory is this: when a loved one is lost only partially, the ambiguity, coupled with loss, creates a powerful barrier to both coping and grieving. There are no familiar rituals for guiding behavior and bringing people together in support of your loss, but there is real and deep sadness. The confusion and lack of support for ambiguous loss leads to depression, anxiety, and family fights and rifts. Close relationships erode, and you are further isolated.

What looks like depression is often sadness; what looks like anxiety is often the immense stress and confusion that comes from not being able to fix the situation. Family conflict often results. Isolation increases. In this milieu, it is no wonder that so many caregivers suffer from complicated and unresolved grief. If you grieve too soon, you feel disloyal to the ill person, or others criticize you. Grief is not denied or repressed, but simply blocked by social, religious, or family taboos against grieving before death has occurred.

By using the lens of ambiguous loss, professionals and caregivers can view grief and loss in more nuanced terms. How does this view help build resiliency? When we look back at how experts understood grief in earlier times, we can see that they did not yet have the relational losses of dementia in mind.

Grief, Officially

Because diagnostic manuals focus primarily on abnormal grief, I go to the dictionary to find a definition of normal grief. Here, grief is defined as "mental anguish" or "deep sorrow caused by bereavement."[3] Bereavement is defined as being "deprived."[4] There is no mention of a time limit or distorted reactions. Medically, however, grief is defined by how long it lasts and by its symptoms—depression, ambivalence, guilt, self-doubt, physical ailments, preoccupation with the lost or deceased, and an inability to function as one did before the loss. As I noted earlier, when such reactions last longer than a few months, ranging from two to six months, one's grief is defined as pathological.

Such definitions of grief are unfair to people whose loved ones have dementia. A definition that focuses on symptoms cannot take into account the context and the type of loss a friend or family member is facing. Experts already know that grief is more difficult when a loss results from an unexpected death (for example, due to suicide or homicide) or is out of synchrony (for example, when a child dies). Yet the grief that results when a beloved person has dementia is not yet officially recognized as exceptional; its complexities are not yet recognized as normal. Therein lies the poor fit between the formal diagnosis of grief and the reality

27

of the mental anguish and deep sorrow you feel when dementia deprives you of what you had.

Getting Over It: An Impossible Idea

For decades in the realm of grief and loss, the assumption was that if mourners couldn't get over a loss within a relatively short period of time (three to six months), there was something wrong with them. This view stems from the work of psychiatrist Erich Lindemann, who in 1944 wrote about his treatment of survivors and the relatives of victims of the tragic Cocoanut Grove Nightclub fire in Boston, where 492 young people died, trapped by a locked door.[5]

Lindemann saw the delayed and repressed mourning of survivors and relatives as pathological, thus solidifying his idea of unresolved grief as personal illness. Although Lindemann's view of grief still holds with many therapists today, he clearly did not consider the unavoidable long-term loss and grief a person experiences when a loved one is cognitively impaired.

Trauma experts, however, may come closer to understanding the kind of grief that dementia causes. Researchers such as Marten deVries and Bessel van der Kolk tell us that grief reactions are more likely to be complicated when "the loss is unexpected, is traumatic, or occurs at times of uncertainty, each of which aggravates the disruption of familiar patterns."[6] Certainly the losses from dementia fit that bill. But here's the rub: the professionals you work with, although they mean well, may still be thinking about Lindemann's definition of normal grief, which means that they'll think you should get over it and move on. This puts you at a disadvantage. You cannot get over sadness or complete your grief process because the losses from your loved one's dementia continue, sometimes for years. Through no fault of your own, sadness becomes chronic.

Grief: A Messy and Unending Process

In 1969, Elisabeth Kübler-Ross developed her five stages of grief: denial, anger, bargaining, depression, and acceptance.[7] What people tend to forget, however, is that Kübler-Ross's stages were not meant for families experiencing the death of a loved one; they were meant for the dying person.[8] Perhaps the Kübler-Ross stage theory of grieving caught on so fast because, according to writer Meghan O'Rourke, "it made loss sound controllable. The trouble is that it turns out largely to be a fiction."[9] Neat formulas like this one become popular because the list of what to expect is so clear and helps us feel in control when things go awry. Unfortunately, loss and grief are much messier processes. In the last nine years of her life, Kübler-Ross suffered from a series of debilitating strokes. She maintained that death was a good experience—but not if it took this long. Her own stages to death were complicated and untidy.[10]

For example, researcher George Bonanno graphs what he calls the oscillations (ups and downs) of grief over time, and we see that these oscillations occur farther apart over time.[11] Grief doesn't go away; it just visits us less often. In my own case, I still grieve for my sister, who died fourteen years ago. When her children called me recently, desperately trying to make the right decision as their father lay at death's door, my immediate thought was *What would my sister want me to say?* I imagined a conversation with her, but her loss became painfully real for me once again. Is this abnormal grief? No. It's the reality of grief's ups and downs.

The ups and downs are real, but ideally they occur farther and farther apart over time, even though they never stop completely. We may prefer neat stages so that we can stop the pain of loss, but grief is not something we can finish altogether. Unlike what the early experts said, you don't have to "get over it."[12] The goal is to live with grief—and to be at peace with that.

More recently, some of us in this field of loss and grief have looked beyond just individual symptoms to study the *context* of grief, or its social environment. In that group is social work professor Kenneth Doka, who coined the term "disenfranchised grief."[13] In your context, being disenfranchised means that socially, you have no permission to grieve. There is no sitting Shiva or wake for a loved one who is still alive. Family or community stoicism—the expectation that one must keep a stiff upper lip—can also cause disenfranchisement. In these situations, mourning and the shedding of tears are unacceptable. Yet dementia creates a loss that is painfully sad. This is precisely the time when you need people around you, bringing food to share and kind words so that you don't to have to bear your loss alone.

■ ■

Given this brief history and update, you can see the poor fit between traditional ideas about loss and grief and your situation. If you are depressed or anxious or have medical issues, talk with your doctor or medical provider or clergy member about what you have lost due to the dementia and to the caregiving you have had to do. It's important that professionals not mistake the sadness of grieving for depression: the interventions differ. For depression, you may need medication; for sadness and grief, you need human connection and the opportunity to grieve in your own way, whenever you feel like it, without criticism, and with the support of comforting others.

Grieving Along the Way

When you're living with dementia, waiting to grieve until it's all over is not reasonable, for that may mean years of holding back the tears. Instead, give yourself permission to grieve along the way, whenever you notice a new loss, small or large.

One woman sent a paper crane out to sea each time she noticed a new loss from her husband's dementia. Another lit candles at her place of worship, another wrote poems, another wrote in her journal, and yet another gathered the family each time there was a new loss, to feel the comfort of children and grandchildren around her—wonderful evidence of the family's continuity. Emma did it yet another way.

Emma was the wife of an elderly man with advanced Alzheimer's disease. When our research team first met with her, she was highly distraught. She told us that her husband wanted sex all the time, but he no longer knew who she was. She said it was like having sex with a stranger, and she didn't think this was right. She was at her wits' end.

A few months later, when we saw her again, she seemed calmer. We asked what had changed. She told us that a solution had just suddenly come to her one day. She went into the bedroom and, with sadness and tears, took off her wedding ring and tucked it away in her jewelry box. After doing this, she said, she knew better how to cope with her ill husband's behavior. She no longer saw him as her sexual partner but as someone she loved dearly and would care for "until death do us part."

Just as she had done with their children years ago, she set boundaries. She moved him to a separate bedroom. Her feelings of obligation to have sex with her husband lessened, but she made sure his other needs were met.

Not only did her stress level lower, but surprisingly so did his. As she became calmer, he did also. Years later, just after her husband died, she went back to her jewelry box, took out her wedding ring, and placed it back on her finger.

I have never forgotten what she said next. "Now I was really a widow, not just a widow waiting to happen."

Symbols such as wedding rings help us and others understand the status of a relationship. But as Emma found, such symbols can also be confusing when there is dementia. Although some outsiders may not understand what Emma did, it allowed her to grieve the part of her relationship that was gone and to take joy in the person who was still here.

Like Emma, many of you are dealing alone in unique ways with complicated grief and loss. Tell other family members and friends about what calms you and what does not. You also need your own doctor or medical provider. Tell him about the reality of your life. If he won't listen, ask for someone else who will. Tell him you are sad, but that there is good reason for it: someone you love has dementia. If you are sleep deprived, tell him why. It's not a medical insomnia but a reaction to nightly disturbances as your loved one wakens and wanders. It's being afraid to sleep for fear that something bad will happen if you doze off. (And it could.) Professionals as well as family members need help in knowing about the complexity of your losses and what is going on around you. Many have no idea.

✿ *Ideas for Reflection and Discussion* ✿

* Not all losses are ambiguous (and unclear), but those that are can create complications that make grieving more difficult.

* Complicated loss creates complicated grief, but the pathology is not due to any personal weakness.

* Whereas the community recognizes and supports one's grief after a death in the family, there are as yet no supports or acknowledgments of ambiguous losses. In fact, there may be criticism if you grieve too early.

* The ambiguity of not knowing for sure if your loved one is here or gone can be a barrier to both coping and grieving. Both processes become frozen by the ambiguity.

* Traditional ideas about abnormal grief must be reevaluated to include the loss and grief of dementia.

* Grieving for someone who is still alive but no longer the person he or she used to be is useful and necessary for your well-being.

✧ Exchange ideas with other caregivers about how to grieve along the way; share ideas about what symbols and rituals might help in this process. What works for you?

✧ But remember, do the grieving *your* way.

3

Stress, Coping, and Resiliency

Beyond coping or problem solving, resilience involves positive transformation and growth.

— FROMA WALSH, STRENGTHENING FAMILY RESILIENCE, SECOND EDITION, 2006, p. x.

Before we can cope with a problem, we need to know what it is. More specifically, we need to be aware of its complexity. Caregiving itself is not the problem, but stress can make it so. The goal is to understand what is causing you more stress so that you and other family members can work to lower it.

Researchers tell us that the primary stresses of caregiving are physical, psychological, emotional, social, and financial.[1] From my observation, loneliness and isolation are central. There are, however, significant differences among caregivers depending on gender, age, and culture—and thus differences in how they cope.

Caregiver Differences

To help assess your own situation, here's what you might call a mini-course to review what researchers have found. We'll begin by looking at the differences in caregiver gender, age, and race and ethnicity, and in coping styles.

Gender

Worldwide, women still predominate as caregivers. When anyone in the family, young or old, needs care, it is primarily mothers, wives, daughters, daughters-in-law, and sisters who provide that care. In the case of Alzheimer's disease, many adult daughters are the caregivers.[2]

Today there are increasing numbers of male caregivers,[3] but women still handle the most difficult and isolating caregiving tasks (feeding, bathing, toileting, and dressing), whereas males are more likely to help with managing finances and arranging for care.[4] Because the hands-on work is so isolating, this difference in the type of work might explain why female caregivers are more likely than male caregivers to report being stressed, anxious, and depressed.[5]

Age

In regard to age, the majority of caregivers for all kinds of illness are between thirty-five and sixty-four years old; the typical caregiver is a forty-six-year-old woman.[6] Of those caring for someone sixty-five or older, the average age is sixty-three years, but note this: one out of three of these caregivers are in fair to poor health.[7]

Although researchers find that older caregivers are at high risk, adult daughters who are caregivers are also at risk because they are often taking care of their own children while also taking care of their parents. When younger caregivers have this double duty, there is little time left for meeting their own needs, and it can threaten their own relationships.

Race and Ethnicity

Race and ethnicity also influence the stresses that caregivers report. African American caregivers report less stress and depression and more rewards than white caregivers.[8] However, Hispanic and Asian American caregivers exhibit more depression than their white counterparts.[9]

Who gives care also varies. Among people age seventy and over who need care, whites most likely receive it from a spouse, Hispanics from their adult children, and African Americans from a nonfamily member. Clearly, more research needs to focus on cultural differences; we can learn from each other about what keeps caregivers healthy and strong.

Coping Style—and Gender Again

Men and women tend to use different coping styles: men use more problem-focused coping, whereas women use more emotion-focused coping. What's important to lowering your stress level is that you feel you have some influence over managing the situation.[10] How you see your effectiveness as a problem solver will influence the effectiveness of the coping style you select.[11]

If you are usually self-directed and self-sufficient and generally feel effective, your coping is also likely to be effective. However, when dementia takes over your life, it isn't easy to remain self-directed and independent. (Chapter Seven offers guidelines for how to do this.)

This brings us back to the issue of gender. Aside from the predominance of females in caregiving, something about women, researchers tell us, makes them more vulnerable than men to the stress of caregiving. Is it due to their coping style, which tends to be more emotionally based? Would the problem-solving style of coping (emphasizing judgment and reasoning) most often used by male caregivers be more effective for female caregivers as well? These are questions worth considering.

In my clinical work, I encourage all caregivers, female and male, to use some of both styles. Use *cognitive coping* when you need to make a decision, solve a problem, and do precise tasks, such as managing medications and appointments. For these, judgment and reasoning

40

are essential. Use *emotion-based coping* to acknowledge feelings—sadness, anger, helplessness, and hopelessness. Talking with a trusted friend or professional can help, but so might listening to poetry or music, or finding some relaxation or sleep.

Perhaps because I'm a woman, or perhaps because I'm a psychotherapist, I value emotion-based coping. Music calms the stresses of my day. Films have always felt like therapy, a two-hour escape into fantasy. Reading is a soothing pleasure, actually a treat, when I can do it undisturbed. And more recently, yoga calms both my body and mind.

I realize of course that you are restricted as a caregiver, but it is nevertheless important to find something that works for you to soothe emotions. Over the years, caregivers have told me what works for them, and the list is varied: piano playing, going to church or synagogue, singing, continuing work outside the home, playing cards with a friend, dining with a friend, participating in a reading group, watching television, reading poetry, knitting, golfing once a week with the guys, praying, meditating, exercising, going out with the girls, and of course getting a good night's sleep. Find something to soothe your emotions at home as well as outside of your home and with others. You need to get out now and then just to find yourself again.

Although I so value emotion-based coping, anyone who knows me realizes quickly that I also use cognitive

41

strategies. I am an information junkie and never make decisions without searching for other options. I make lists, set goals, and use logic to solve problems. Until writing this, I haven't really thought about how I cope, but now I see that I use both styles—perhaps getting the best of both worlds, as the saying goes.

Try this too. Think about which style of coping you use and when. If you lean more in one direction, ask yourself if you might lower your stress by using more variety in how you cope and manage. With either coping style, however, know that your effectiveness depends on being positive—not ignoring despair, but believing you can manage the situation even though it's difficult.

Being positive doesn't mean you can't have a good cry now and then. Or as one caregiver told me, "When I'm at my wits' end, I go out into the garage, get into the car, make sure the windows are up—and scream." This was her way of calming herself without frightening her husband. She understood herself well enough to know when she needed to release some tension—and found a functional way to do it.

Positive coping means assessing your feelings regularly. Emma, whom you heard about in the previous chapter, is an example of someone who assessed her feelings and then acted to relieve her stress. She built on the positive—like the old song that says, "accentuate the positive, eliminate the negative." She didn't feel sorry for herself, nor was she stuck in wishful thinking. She was aware of her feelings, which then motivated her to make the necessary changes.

Barriers to Coping and Managing

Aside from the influence of one's coping style, gender, race, and ethnicity on who gives care and how one copes and manages, there are barriers that can make caregiving more stressful than it needs to be. Most are unnecessary and could be changed if the family or community made the decision to do so. Although you may be experiencing other difficulties, the impediments I address here are family conflict, stress pileup, negative judgment, isolation, cultural stigma, rigid perceptions, and ambiguity anxiety.

Family Conflict

A barrier to managing stress, and one of the most harmful to caregivers, is family conflict. At the extreme, I see caregivers become outcasts in their own families just because of old or new disagreements. If for no other reason than to lift that additional stress from an already stressed caregiver, it is worthwhile to solicit the help of a family psychologist or family therapist to help heal the conflict. Stepfamilies in particular may need family therapy, especially if a late-life marriage pits the children against the caregiver who is a relative newcomer in their family.[12] Trust issues usually cannot be settled without

43

the help of outside professionals to clear up the issues under question and reconcile the hostile relationships.

But even families who have gotten along well in the past will predictably disagree and argue when there is ambiguity about an illness or its care. Few realize that a family environment of conflict predicts caregiver depression. Reducing conflict is obviously important if you want the family caregiver to stay healthy.

One piece of good news is that a caregiver's perception of her or his burden actually lowers when other family members show their appreciation.[13] We shouldn't need researchers to tell us this. Showing appreciation is an intervention that should be so easy to do. I often wonder if near or faraway relatives realize that it's in their best interest to say "thank you" to the on-site caregiver. They should call, or send flowers, money, or food—and take over for a week or even just a few days so that the caregiver can take a vacation from an exhausting job. Caregivers tell me they feel hurt when no one calls or notices. They feel abandoned. But to caregivers I say, let your family and friends know that you need help. Ask them outright to do a particular task or to relieve you. Waiting for them to volunteer is frustrating and often fruitless—so ask for what you need. Be assertive. Blame it on me. Blame it on your doctor.

Family teamwork is essential to caregiver health—thus my recommendation of family meetings (even if some participants join in by speakerphone or Skype). When family members are tempted to turn on each other in times of stress and difficulty, it's useful for all to remember that they have a common enemy—the dementia—and to pitch in to help, one way or another. More will be said in Chapter Seven about how to do this.

Stress Pileup

To add to your pile of stress, dementia's loss is, as we've seen, not a one-time event. Over time—usually a long time—there is a cascade of losses, like a tumbling mountain river. For the patient, there is the loss of memory, the loss of being able to travel, the loss of being able to walk, the loss of knowing anyone, the loss of continence, and, near the end, the loss of being able to swallow food or water—all representing more obstacles to cope with.

For you, or any caregiver, there's likely to be the loss of your loved one as he or she used to be, the loss of your relationship as it was, the loss of the basic need to have an undisturbed night's sleep, the loss of your dreams and goals, the loss of leisure time that you expected to have in this stage of your life, and the loss of your independence and control over your own life. This stream of losses understandably wears caregivers down, but outsiders often don't see this. In my practice, I hear many stories of cascading ambiguous losses, but often there is also a pileup of several *different* ambiguous losses at one time—for example, the losses experienced by an adult

45

daughter caring for her elderly father with dementia *and* her young child with autism, or those of an adult daughter whose mother is being moved to a nursing home just as a child is moving away to go to college. Such multiple losses only add to the onslaught. Professionals, as well as the general public, often miss this complexity of stress in a caregiver's life.

Negative Judgment

Perhaps one of the unstated burdens on caregivers is the judgment they receive from others—relatives as well as professionals. That caregivers are usually aware of these judgments only adds to their stress. In my practice, I have often been told by caregivers that they shed so many tears along the way, there will be none left for the funeral. I tell them not to worry if others criticize them for having no tears left, because they've already grieved plenty along the way. This is typical for long-term dementia. Be like Teflon: don't let the negative judgment stick to you.

Professionals, too, may judge caregivers and see them in a negative light. A longtime caregiver who attended one of my workshops—I'll call her Helen—told me, "The doctor told me I am in denial when he gives me information, but I'm not. I am just putting the bad news in my pocket, so I can take it out when I can more easily bear the pain of it. He tells me that the brain is damaged and won't get better. I act like I don't hear, but actually I do. I just tuck the bad news away for later."

Helen asked me if I thought her method of coping was really denial. "No," I said. "You seem to know what you're doing. In the short term, denial can actually be a helpful way of coping—especially when you are aware that you are using it to delay, for a short time, some very bad news. In fact, you found a very good way to manage the stress of painful news." When the news is shocking and things aren't going your way, you need time to take it in.

Isolation

Caregivers for dementia patients are often isolated. This is because they tend to be older and often vulnerable, and thus less able to go out or travel. As a result, they spend less time with other family members and may give up vacations, hobbies, and other social activities. Isolation leads to higher burden and depression for caregivers—and in turn, this leads to more behavioral problems in the person who has dementia.[14] In other words, one's retreat from social activities has a negative effect on *both* caregiver and patient. Because this point is so important I will say it yet another way: avoid isolation with some social activity; it's essential for the well-being of both you *and* the person you care for.

Cultural Stigma

Another barrier for coping is the stigma of dementia. There are important cultural differences regarding how dementia is perceived or stigmatized. Researcher Peggye Dilworth-Anderson confirms that family caregiving processes are influenced by culture and ethnicity, which determine the meaning of caregiving for a particular family and who will do the work and how.[15]

Also, from studies in various cultures, researchers find that (1) female caregivers are more at risk; (2) white caregivers report more depression than African American caregivers—perhaps because of how they perceive their task and dementia itself (whites are more likely to see dementia as stigma, whereas African Americans see it as part of the circle of life); and (3) Asian cultures show a greater sense of duty to care for elderly family members but also more need for privacy due to stigmatization, and thus offer less social and emotional support for caregivers.[16]

The scores of burden and depression for Chinese and Korean caregivers were, therefore, higher than for Western caregivers.[17] Although Asian cultures have traditionally prescribed filial piety—a sense of responsibility to care for one's elders—there is, at the same time, a cultural stigma against dementia patients, which results in the isolation of caregivers.[18] This is not good. More recently, however, I read that South Koreans now train their children to be with people who have dementia. This is a good example of social change to acknowledge and support an aging population.[19]

Positive support from one's family, friends, and community is critical to a caregiver's health. If you are a relative or a friend of a caregiver, try to enlighten at least one other person in your community who could help you teach others. People need to know that stigmatizing dementia patients also harms caregivers—and society needs caregivers desperately.

Rigid Perceptions

Although stressors may differ, each of you will have your own perceptions about your loved one's dementia and what the situation means to you. Whether I meet with individuals, couples, families, or groups of families, I always ask this question: "What does this situation mean to you?" Rigid thinking blocks coping.

Indeed, answers often vary within couples and families, but it's all right for family members to see the situation differently. When a loss remains unclear—as it does with dementia—people understandably disagree on what it means. I tell them to simply listen to each other's views. The process is not about a right answer versus a wrong answer, or normal versus abnormal. It's about trying to make sense of an ambiguous loss, and each individual does that in a unique way. The correctness of your interpretation of the situation doesn't matter unless, of course, your viewpoint is life threatening to yourself or others. Some people cannot tolerate ambiguity and become dangerously

49

desperate in these situations. In such cases, treatment is needed immediately.

In my clinical work, I see people who struggle dogmatically with the ambiguity of dementia. Early on, they tend to see the situation as one of two extremes: (1) denying that anything is wrong or (2) seeing the ill person as already gone or no longer human (just a shell). As I've mentioned earlier, neither of these two extreme perceptions is functional. Reality lies in the middle ground.

Ambiguity Anxiety

Coping with dementia requires us to live with shades of gray. An accountant whose father had dementia could not. The ambiguity terrorized him. He said, "I can deal with my father as long as I consider him a piece of furniture and don't bump into him." I was stunned. But I have learned that many people are so terrorized by dementia that they decide it's over when in fact it's not. This is ambiguity anxiety. You can't stand it, so you concoct clarity artificially.

Ultimately, we all have to wrestle with these questions: What's my tolerance for ambiguity? Can I be at ease with a loved one who is both here and gone at the same time? Can I stay in a less than perfect relationship?

The accountant could not. But his young son could, and it was he who over time coaxed his father back to the nursing home, even though the old man had lost all memory. Visiting the grandfather together, father and son grew closer, and the accountant learned to increase his tolerance for ambiguity—not an easy thing in his profession. What serves as good coping and problem solving in one's professional life may be disastrous in more intimate family life.

People with dementia need our touch and the sound of our voices even if they don't always know who we are. We can learn to handle that. Our humanity depends on it. We can indeed give to someone who is no longer able to give back, at least intentionally. In close relationships, we should not always expect the ledger to be balanced.

Relationships often are not perfectly reciprocal. Giving to someone unconditionally, without expecting anything back, is the ultimate test of ego and grace—and it can provide us with a measure of satisfaction and peace that eases our own pain.

Consider Ruth, whose husband, we learned in the previous chapter, had a stroke followed by dementia. She was still caring for her husband and had realized long ago that dementia is not a one-time loss. His diagnosis was only the first of many. Her losses cascaded over the years—the loss of sexual intimacy, the loss of his knowing who she was, the loss of her leisure time with friends as his dependency on her increased, and so on.

Each paralyzed her for a time until she found her footing again and figured out how to manage the next step. Grief was eased when a support group told her that her sadness was normal. Her support group was invaluable, and several members became close friends. Being with others who were "in the same boat" helped her find her strength again after each new blow. Talks and books by experts gave her information that helped her manage and make important decisions. Listening to music, writing poetry, and attending church lifted her spirits so that she could keep going. Her journey as a caregiver lasted five years.[20]

Resiliency in caregivers is more common than most experts think. It just appears in different forms. It is essential for all of us to understand why caregivers differ—to know who is most vulnerable and why, and to learn of the different management styles—and to understand that there is more than one right way to perform this role. The important point for you, however, is that barriers to managing your stress must be removed. For that, the larger community, if not society at large, must help. With others, try to advocate in your community for more public education about dementia so that its terror will not isolate you and your loved one.

⫷ *Ideas for Reflection and Discussion* ⫸

❋ To cope and stay resilient on this journey with dementia, list the specific stressors you face. Once you comprehend what the problem is and its complexity, you can begin to manage and cope with it.

❋ Caregiving stress can be physical, emotional, spiritual, financial, and social, but there are also differences in gender, age, race, and ethnicity that influence caregivers. What fits for you?

❋ Rigid cultural rules about gender roles overload female caregivers and stigmatize males, who are increasingly taking up the caregiver role.

❋ Providing you with information to help you cope is often called "psychoeducation." It is one of the most effective forms of intervention.

❋ In addition to information, human connection helps you cope. Find a friend, a support group—people who can be fully present for you.

❋ Feeling confident in your ability to manage stress and solve problems helps you cope; that is, *believing* you can do this actually helps.

✿ Losses continue to cascade over time with dementia, so both coping and grieving processes are ongoing. This causes unusually high stress for even the strongest persons and families.

✿ Barriers to coping and managing stress often can be changed with public education as well as with the help of enlightened professionals.

✿ Being resilient means more than just recovering from adversity. It means gaining new strength from the experience. In the case of loving someone who has dementia, resilience means becoming more comfortable with the stress and anxiety caused by the ambiguity and having no closure.

4

The Myth of Closure

I have gradually been coming to feel that the door is no longer shut and bolted.

—C. S. LEWIS, *A GRIEF OBSERVED, 1961, p. 58*

Since the 1960s, perhaps due to frequent usage by pop psychologists, journalists, and television personalities, the phrase *finding closure* has become commonplace. Many in American society use it to indicate that one's grief has ended. The goal then becomes one of getting over loss and moving on.

I find this way of thinking offensive and steeped in the values of a culture that not only denies death but also assumes that the loss of a loved one will have a clearly demarcated ending. Dementia is proof that closure is a myth. Just ask those who live with it.

I first learned about the myth of closure from families of the *physically* missing. In 1974, I was a doctoral student doing a research project at the Center for Prisoner of War

55

Studies in San Diego, interviewing wives of military pilots who had been declared missing in action in Vietnam. Back then, the families had no knowledge of whether their loved ones were alive or dead, and most of them had to live the rest of their lives without knowing.[1] As I interviewed the wives of the missing pilots, they often talked about *The Little Prince* and how that story had given them comfort. I had thought the book was for children, but then discovered that it was about a downed pilot and the struggle to find meaning when a loved one disappears.[2] Storytellers—such as Antoine de Saint-Exupéry and C. S. Lewis—show us metaphorically that the door to loss does not have to be, as Lewis wrote, "shut and bolted."

Today, decades later, when I reread Saint-Exupéry's little book, and perhaps because I am older, with too many friends downed by dementia, I think about the *psychologically* missing. Saint-Exupéry writes about loving a person (the little prince in this case) who is still here, but rapidly slipping away: "I realized clearly that something extraordinary was happening. I was holding him close in my arms as if he were a little child; and yet it seemed to me that he was rushing headlong toward an abyss from which I could do nothing to restrain him."[3]

But then he goes on: "There is nothing sad about old shells."[4] In my work, I often hear family members refer to loved ones with dementia as being "like a shell of their former selves." "There is no one there." "She is nothing but a shell, so I consider her dead." But Saint-Exupéry tells us that it's okay to love an old shell—and I agree.

Loving someone who is only a shell of his or her former self is indeed commendable. And it's a "real matter of consequence."[5] People who live with dementia know this. But not everyone does. If the community sees no merit in caring for someone who has become more "like a shell," then those who do this difficult work are more likely to become invisible.

Although we prefer a relationship with someone who is fully present, we discover that it's possible to stay in a relationship without such presence. Partial presence can be sufficient. We don't need perfection to continue caring.

I think of my long-departed maternal grandmother, Elsbeth, every time I see her rose gold pin in my jewelry box. She brought it with her in 1911 when she emigrated from Switzerland to New Glarus, Wisconsin. She always wore it when she dressed up to go to church or a concert. Later on, in her seventies and diagnosed with what was then called senile dementia, she gradually changed into a woman I no longer knew. She was a shell of her former self, but I still loved her. I remembered how she had rocked me as a child, and then my own babies, while singing the same Swiss-German lullabies. Seeing that rose gold pin, the symbol of her better days, comforted me as a young mother back then when the dementia took her away—and still today when I am now a grandmother myself. Even after her death so long ago, there's still no need to close that door.

For me, it was a rose gold pin, but for Saint-Exupéry's pilot, it was the golden grain that reminded him of his loved one's golden hair: "The grain, which is also golden, will bring me back the thought of you. And I shall love to listen to the wind in the wheat."[6]

When we love certain people, whether they are partially or fully gone, we still remember our relationship and how they were in the good days. There can never truly be closure. It's normal to remember the past—with loved ones in their prime—even though we are fully aware that things have changed.

Where Did the Idea of Closure Come From?

Philosophers, early therapists, and now neuroscientists support the idea that human beings prefer exact solutions. In the case of loss, that means closure. Your loved one is either here or not here. No in-between. Although your cultural beliefs influence whether you value closure and, if so, how you may find it—whether through official death certificates, visions, or dreams—it must be deeply distressing not to know if your loved one is here or gone. Yet if he or she has dementia, you have to live with this lack of clarity. Closure for you is a myth.

In the 1970s, Gestalt therapist Fritz Perls, a contemporary of my mentor, Carl Whitaker, wrote about the "law of closure." Perls saw closure as the human tendency for self-organization, completion, and symmetry.[7] Did he mean that life was supposed to be neat and tidy?

Although you may yearn for closure, it's really unattainable when someone you love has dementia. The whole of your relationship is built on the duality of absence and presence. There is no completion or symmetry here, and the imbalance can become a source of great stress for you.

Today researchers are confirming that human beings do indeed seek tidiness. Neuropsychologists have found that the brain doesn't like ambiguity and that when faced with it, there is great cognitive effort to find a decisive or clear solution.[8] Cognitive psychologists agree that the human mind inherently tries to eliminate ambiguity. People yearn for a definitive solution or conclusion, referred to as "cognitive coping."[9]

Because a neat and tidy ending is not possible with dementia, you might instead lower your stress level by finding *meaning*, not closure. That is, find meaning in the ambiguity instead of fighting it. (More will be said about finding meaning in Chapters Seven, Eight, and Nine.)

There is no way we can know today whether or not Whitaker and Perls would agree that messy and unclear relationships are painful. Yet I do know from clinical observations and from visiting my own elders and my mentor, Carl Whitaker, after he suffered a stroke and lingered on, that expecting a neat and tidy closure to a loved one's life is the real absurdity.

Very likely, the early pioneers were not thinking of dementia, but they did recognize the paradoxes in human relationships. I now see new meaning in Perls's famous Gestalt Prayer: "You are you and I am I, and if by chance we find each other, it's beautiful. If not, it can't be helped."[10] It could be a caregiver's prayer because it takes away guilt and blame. If dementia prevents you and your loved one from finding each other, there is no judgment. It just is what it is.

The problem is that there is more enthusiasm for finding closure than for finding meaning. From medical and mental health professionals to grief experts, friends, and relatives, there is a push, if not a demand, for an absolute end to one's mourning. Anyone who lingers is considered abnormal.

From my observations, it's their chronic sorrow that isolates caregivers.[11] People stay away because such sadness frightens them. The sadness and grief (when no one has died) are not easily understood in a society that denies death, so instead of finding ways to comfort your sadness, others may too often call it depression and do nothing to ease your isolation.

This is how I see it: a culture that values mastery and control will demand closure; a culture that denies death will demand closure; a culture that assumes we can

60

avoid suffering will demand closure; and our own anxiety about death will demand closure. Our intense societal and personal need for closure makes loving someone with dementia an uphill climb. When someone you love has dementia, the challenge is to balance mastery and control with acceptance. (You can read more about this in Chapter Seven.)

Living Without Closure

Although the need for closure may be strong in U.S. society, many people view closure as unnatural and a barrier to healing. For example, I have worked with some Asian American families who intentionally kept a family member present in the form of memorabilia or household altars that honor their loved ones after they had died. I have worked with Mexican American families who looked forward to annual celebrations of the dead and visiting the family gravesite where they would gather to picnic.[12] They were not so anxious about death. No wonder they are offended when well-meaning professionals push for closure.

I saw this after 9/11 while working in Lower Manhattan with immigrant families. They all had loved ones who were missing, and they were in no hurry to end the grieving. I had to fend off journalists who would ask why these families weren't "over it" yet. Although these families were eager to have verification of death, they knew that their grieving would never really end. In fact, most of the families I worked with believed they would meet their loved ones again. They even had conversations with them—as I did with my sister (see Chapter Two). I am a Midwesterner, but I felt camaraderie with the Latino families I met in New York City. I was touched when after several visits with them, their children called me their grandma (abuela) from the Midwest.

Human relationships can indeed transcend time and place. This is an idea that can ease your stress. Think of the past when the present becomes too painful and confusing. And when the future brings even deeper dementia, rather than close the door, try to integrate all of the messiness into a whole—a kind of psychological family of loved ones both here and gone. (More will be said about the psychological family in Chapter Five.)

The Legacy of Ambiguous Loss and No Closure

Although it is rarely acknowledged, the cultural legacy in the United States is one of unresolved loss. The story of slavery and missing family members is among the first.[13] In *The Republic of Suffering*, Harvard historian Drew Gilpin Faust writes about another, when during the Civil War it was common for families of young soldiers never to have proof of death or remains to bury.[14] Bodies were left where they fell or buried in unmarked graves. For most of the country in post–Civil War America, there was no closure. Seldom is this legacy of unresolved loss recognized.[15]

Whether we speak of slavery or of soldiers in unknown graves or abandoned, or of the myriad of other people cut off from their families by wars and immigration or migration, we are a society of people often separated from those we love. Given this history of ambiguous loss, ours is a nation founded on unresolved grief. No wonder so many deny death—and insist on the tidiness of closure.

This legacy of needing to close the door on unresolved loss is still a factor in American culture. Yet until we temper this need for closure, our anxiety about loss will isolate people who are suffering. They will be left alone in their sadness.

The United States is a culture that denies death. This denial, in concert with our historical legacy, now creates more stress for caregivers. Why? People who deny death are more likely to be terrorized by dementia. They stay away.

The Rupture in Meaning

Making sense of a relationship altered by dementia is difficult, as logic and reason come apart. Meaning is ruptured, thus increasing your feelings of helplessness and hopelessness.[16] For you to make sense of this new relationship, your previous ideal of a close relationship—one with balanced roles and clear boundaries[17]—must change.

When an illness has no cure, the only opportunity for regaining balance and control is to see the situation in a new light. If we see the ambiguity as ongoing, it makes sense to let go of the idea of closure. When we know there's a name for what we feel and that our feelings of sadness are normal, it also makes sense to shift gears. When our minds seek normality in the midst of ongoing ambiguity, we can simply define disorder and messiness as normal.

Choosing to embrace rather than resist the ambiguity is, paradoxically, the way to find meaning in it. Learn to live with two opposing ideas—here and gone, present and absent. Talk to your loved ones even when they don't answer; touch and hug them even if they don't return your gestures. Visit when you can as a favor to yourself because this deepens your humanity and increases your tolerance for ambiguity—measures of good mental health.

Sarah faced this challenge. She was a sixty-year-old caregiver whose husband showed signs some years ago of "not being himself." Once affable, he became angry; once reasonable, he was bad tempered. Illness was taking away his beautiful mind. Sarah stopped her professional work and became his full-time caregiver. After he died, she reflected:

> It was harder work than I ever imagined, the
> worst of it being that I was never done. It was like

being on call all the time. I hardly slept that last year. We didn't handle it well all the time. He had always been very independent and proud of it so he often resisted my help. Sometimes I was worn out, and my patience was gone. Yet, we loved each other, and I was committed to him—"till death do us part."

Sarah said that she found meaning in doing the job well and in being able to do the heavy work of caregiving. She helped her husband by managing the tasks of daily life, his personal care, the lifting, the chauffeuring to appointments, and the managing of his medications. She also kept the house going with cooking and cleaning. The satisfaction of accomplishing so much is what got her through each day.

Not every caregiver would find the same meaning Sarah did. No doubt because she was an athletic woman and in good health, she found satisfaction in her endurance and strength. Although she suffered physically at times—losing weight and having some back problems—she was nevertheless resilient enough to continue the hard work.

Sarah cared for her husband for five years and never gave up on her commitment to him. But she also knew early on that something had drastically changed in their relationship. When nothing else made sense, she found meaning in being able to do the work and help him as best she could.

As a person accustomed to solving problems, Sarah needed time to accept the situation. She didn't like to give up her view of an ideal relationship, but eventually she saw her relationship in a new way. She realized that *she* had to change because her husband could not—and the dementia would not.

What Helps?

In cultures where people believe they can always win over adversity, the skill of adaptation or compromise is devalued. But adapt we must, even in mastery-oriented cultures, until scientists can find preventions or treatments for dementia. Meanwhile, we learn from the many who, out of necessity, have discovered how to adapt and stay strong despite unresolved loss.

As you experience the ongoing losses that come with dementia, try to let go of the idea of finding closure; instead, focus on finding meaning in the contradiction and paradox of dementia's absence and presence. Unfortunately, many of us in the field are still influenced by the psychiatric view of Erich Lindemann, who, nearly seventy years ago, told us that if we did the work of grieving well, we could get over it.[18] We could achieve a finite end to the grief. Not so.

Today, researchers and clinicians studying loss find that we can live with grief more easily if we don't try so hard to get over it.[19] And dementia teaches us that grief's door is never completely shut.

For you to stay in control, your goal is to decide *intentionally* to embrace the ambiguity. It's your choice. Remember, you're in charge of your own perceptions and what they mean.

The myth is that healthy people find closure, but the truth is that most of us learn to live with grief. Even after their death, we don't forget the people we've loved and lost—and this brings us to what I call the psychological family, the topic of the next chapter.

《 *Ideas for Reflection and Discussion* 》

As you reflect on these ideas and questions and talk about them with others, consider how they influence your view on closure.

- ❖ Compare your cultural beliefs about loss and closure with others. Ideas about living without closure could be helpful to you now as a caregiver.

- ❖ Do you lean toward seeking mastery and control, or can you at times accept life as it comes?

- ❖ Can you accept that some problems may not be solved or that some illnesses may not be cured in time for your loved one?

- ❖ Are you distressed by ambiguity?

- ❖ Do you need a definitive solution to be calm?

Think about and discuss these two different views:

Absolute Thinking

An absolutist view values certainty and absolute answers; there is a tendency to engage in black-and-white thinking. In regard to dementia, these views are focused on mastering the situation.

* If my will is strong enough, I can handle what I am given to do.

* If I "work through" my grief, I can find closure.

* If I'm moral and work hard, I will avoid suffering.

* If I'm a good person, I should be able to give up my anger and ambivalence.

* If my will is strong enough, I can find closure and move on.

* My loved one is either here or gone; he or she can't be both.

From this perspective, grief is viewed as a rational and linear process: if you work hard, you will get to the end of the steps, find closure, and end the pain and suffering. Although this more Western view of working hard is highly desired and valued when there is a clear problem to solve, some problems (like dementia) have no solution. Until there is a solution, you may be able to lower your stress by expanding your ways of thinking.

Tolerance for Ambiguity

A person who tolerates ambiguity is comfortable with doubt, uncertainty, and shades of gray. Eastern views about loss and grief may be more helpful in living with someone with an incurable dementia.

- ✸ Closure is not desirable or possible.
- ✸ The more you try to forget a loss, the more you'll be preoccupied with it.
- ✸ You don't have to "get over" a loss; you learn to live with it.
- ✸ Absence and presence are relative in all close relationships.
- ✸ There are few absolutes in life.
- ✸ Living with ambiguous loss means accepting paradox.
- ✸ You can see a loved one as both present *and* absent.
- ✸ Loss and suffering are inevitable, especially when you love and attach.
- ✸ Death is a natural part of the circle of life.

From this Eastern perspective, we can more easily accept the paradox of absence and presence. We can live more comfortably with dementia and its ambiguous loss. Feelings of ongoing sadness and grief, ambiguity, and uncertainty are familiar and acceptable. The inability to find closure is not viewed as failure.

5

The Psychological Family

If [people] define things as real, they are real in their consequences.

—W. I. THOMAS, THE CHILD IN AMERICA, 1928, p. 572

A mericans live in one of the most individualistic cultures in the world, yet "a wealth of research documents that when Americans are asked what makes them happy, most cite their close personal relationships with other people."[1] Human connections prevent loneliness and can even stave off illness and sudden death,[2] so when one's family and friends live far away or cannot be supportive, there's a need for what I call a *psychological family*. Although family is commonly thought of as a biological and legal entity, it can also be

71

psychological—an important distinction for caregivers who feel alone. Barbara, a caregiver, sums it up perfectly:

> The psychological family is not a second hand alternative to the biological, but an expansion of it. It is important to have "family" members that are physically close as well as those that can be mentally and spiritually supportive. The term "psychological" covers all these situations—it is the "family" that we choose.

A psychological family, then, is created in your heart and mind. It can be your family of origin, but it can also be intentionally chosen, as psychologist Dorothy Becvar says, as "mental representations of family."[3] It's the people you choose to have with you at your special times, like holidays and celebrations. It's the person or persons you want to talk with in good times and bad. It's someone who truly likes you and is there for you. Your psychological family could be made up of friends, neighbors, a book group, a spiritual congregation—or even other caregivers who understand best what it is you do. Barbara, who was a longtime caregiver for her husband and part of a group, adds:

> We are aware of many instances where some biological family members are not at all helpful or supportive, sometimes even the opposite. Devastating for caregivers, particularly in the early stages of dealing with the disease. This idea of

psychological families, which seems simple and
obvious to some ... offer[s] hope to those that
feel so alone on their journey.

It's not unusual for people to have surrogates or stand-
ins for family—neighborhood kids who are like grandchildren, friends who become like sisters or brothers, and
friends with whom we spend holidays and special events.
When you aren't with your biological family, such proxies
serve a valuable purpose in providing human connection
and social support, something absolutely essential when
you're caring for someone who has dementia.

I encourage you to be creative in shaping your psychological family. To begin, recognize that the structure of
one's family need not be only biological. If biological kin
are physically far away, find ways to stay connected psychologically. Many military and immigrant families do this
by using e-mail, webcams, and telephone to stay in touch
with one another regularly. If loved ones who gave you
support are now deceased, think of them and keep some
symbols of them in your life—a ring, a recipe, a photo, an
item of clothing, a song. Think of them when you need
support. What might they say to encourage you now?
What might you say to them? Psychologically, this can
be comforting. Although we often don't admit it, we may
also talk to them now and then. Many people I see tell me
that having God in their lives helps them feel less alone.

Psychological families can also be created with
like-minded people in similar cultures. Consider

expatriates living abroad; gay and lesbian families who are not accepted by their own kin; parents who have adopted children from a particular foreign country; families in which, for one reason or another, parents and children or sisters and brothers no longer speak and are estranged from one another. And, of course, caregivers who are geographically isolated and alone. For all, the psychological family can be a safety net. Barbara then asks an important question: "Do we choose others *only* because our biological families aren't around? We might not want some of those biological family members in our psychological family anyway. We might need others who are more empathetic and emotionally available."

What caregivers need is human connection, one way or another. You need someone who can be there for you in person or through technology, someone who is present for you physically, symbolically, or spiritually. It may be some or all of those for you. It's up to you to decide.

The Necessity of Close Relationships

From early researchers like Ellen Bercheid (my colleague at the University of Minnesota) to Martin Seligman (the pioneer of positive psychology) to Oprah (we all know who she is), we now know that our well-being is tied to our connections with other people who love and support us.[4]

On the other side, however, the lack of close relationships brings unhappiness—and loneliness, which can lead to physical illness. Caregivers, take heed. Whether it's your family of origin, family of choice, or spiritual family, you need a psychological family whose members are there for you, in good times and bad. Mostly this means being with supportive people in your neighborhood or those in the groups and situations described previously. If, however, you're not able to leave the house, or if you live in a remote area or are otherwise isolated, your psychological family could be a virtual group on the Internet with unrelated people—friends or other caregivers—who become so important that they are family to you.

Barbara makes an important point as she shares her experience:

> The concept of actually physically spending time with supportive people and friends assumes an amount of time that may not be available to many caregivers. One of the most challenging situations is how to maintain a somewhat normal relationship with family and friends—relationships take time. That is what we have the least. Most casual relationships are lost, and others that don't fit into the psychological family are difficult to maintain. So, even with our psychological family members, sometimes only a quick phone call or e-mail is possible. I was with supportive people when I could be, but I was also connected electronically/virtually just as often. It was not an

either/or but both. One wasn't necessarily better
than the other. It just depended on our needs
and time. (One characteristic of our psychological
family members was that there seemed to be
no "relationship needs." They were there for
my husband and me with no expectations—
what a gift.)

What a caregiver needs in a family, regardless of its
source, is what researchers find necessary for all human
health: affection, caring, reassurance of worth, advice and
guidance, proximity (visiting frequently or being physically nearby), coping assistance, nurturance, reliable asso-
ciations, and tangible assistance.[5] What you *don't* need is
criticism, judgment, discouragement, ridicule, or isolation.

My First Experience with the Psychological Family

I grew up with a real family and a psychological family.
My father came to the United States in 1929, an unfortunate time because of the Great Depression. He had
planned to study here for two years, then return to his
homeland for a career and marriage. But it was a terrible
time for a young man on his way up. The opportunities to
work were nonexistent, and he was unable to earn money
for his return. He was stuck. He eventually found work
on a farm in southeastern Wisconsin, fell in love with the
girl next door, and started a family.

From the time I can remember, he had two families: his mother and siblings in Switzerland, about whom he talked often, and my mother and us children on a farm in Wisconsin. He worked hard to recreate Swiss life there with music, food, celebrations, costumes, literature, language, and stories—all ways of keeping his faraway family in his heart and mind. He was proud of his American citizenship (I still remember how we celebrated when he became a citizen), but he was always torn, not patriotically, but psychologically, because his Swiss family was out of reach. Back then, with the economic depression and then World War II, visits were impossible.

My father's experience as an immigrant, and mine as a first-generation American, were not unusual. This country is made up of many people who come from someplace else. Homesickness and longing for the family members left behind are common. For many, relatives living far away become part of their psychological families, providing comfort and stability when the going gets rough.

Some time after both my parents had died, I was packing up their house and found my father's wallet in an old bureau. Along with the usual identification cards, there was a surprise that brought tears to my eyes. Deep down in his wallet, in what was then called the "secret pocket," I found an old brown photo. It was of his hometown, Burgdorf, Switzerland. The scene was of his home, his church, and the steep bluffs, where, he told me so many times, he loved to play with his brothers. This

77

old photo told me that even though he left this happy home in 1929, my father carried this symbol of his Swiss home and his psychological family with him until his death sixty-one years later.[6]

I had always known that my father was yearning for his family and home back in Switzerland, and here was proof, hidden away in the old wallet he always carried. His mother and siblings were indeed his psychological family—the one in his heart and mind—and with him always for the rest of his life in America. He was a wonderful father to me, but I knew his mind and heart were often with them. I can still hear him in his broken English telling young immigrants that if they stayed in the United States longer than three months, they would never again know where home was.

At an early age, I felt the presence of my father's psychological family—and it was from this longing that I learned early that there was such a thing as ambiguous loss. When family members are beloved but out of reach, we keep them present in other ways. One way or another, we stay connected.

Who Is in Your Psychological Family?

When you care for someone with dementia, it's essential to know who your family is, because you need extra support—real and willingly given. Whether your psychological family is actual, virtual, spiritual, divine, or a combination thereof, it is essential for your health and well-being.

In therapy sessions, when I ask people who their psychological family is, they often have the answer at their fingertips. They know right away who's in and who's out. Over time, of course, their perceptions of family change with births, deaths, and marriages. Yet neither biology nor a marriage license is a sufficient "qualification" for getting inside a family—or being able to stay in it. Many of the clients I see have been cut off by family members who, because of disagreements or conflict, no longer speak to them.[7] The Amish call this *shunning*, a rare and intentional punishment, but I also see a version of this with caregivers who are left to endure the stress alone.

It's important for you to know who's on the family team. Who is acting like family to ease your load? Who's there for you when you need help? Who's there for you when you need someone to listen, to drive, to run errands, to just play a game of Scrabble, or to help around the house so you can go to a movie or shop? When a family member has dementia, there's no time to coddle the slackers. You need to know who has your back, and if biological family members are unwilling or too far away, seek support elsewhere. What caregivers need is someone—or several people—who can be unconditionally supportive. Like a good sister or a good brother.

Barbara tells me she really appreciates the "no time to coddle the slackers" remark, having spent "many hours in support groups discussing the frustration, hurt, and anger of caregivers who try to make their biological family members understand. At least in the beginning, it doesn't even seem to be so much about support as it is about believing and accepting the condition." She continues, "Much caregiver anxiety seems to be spent here—understanding how to build a psychological family and how to give up on the slackers. That might really help."

In my therapy office, I have a print from Picasso's Blue Period. It's called *The Tragedy*. It depicts a family—two parents and child—painted in cold blue, standing apart from each other, each with his or her arms around himself or herself, as if shivering from the cold. No one is touching, talking, or making eye contact with the others.[8] You feel the cold and loneliness. I keep it behind a shelf (because it's so depressing) and only bring it out when I need to illustrate to a family how disengaged and cut off they are. This painting illustrates a caregiver's nightmare: family members so preoccupied with their own lives that the caregiver is not noticed, touched, thanked, or contacted. Theirs, then, is a family with nobody in it.

To stave off loneliness and to have help when needed, you have to know who is—and who will be—there for you. It's not always who you think it is. Other people can become proxies, offering you the support your own family might otherwise give if it were not for problems of mobility and distance or of conflict or denial. It's actually a liberating idea.

Even as you build your psychological family, you most likely will still feel loyal to your biological family, even when they can't meet your needs. That's good. You're using both-and thinking—and you're not succumbing to absolutes and blaming. Family members may live thousands of miles away, or they just may not understand your situation. If they don't understand the pain of ambiguous loss and its strain on you, they will lack the empathy you need. It's not a cause for reproach, but it *is* an urgent matter of public education for the benefit of caregiver health. (More will be said about empathy later.)

Here's where others can help. If you aren't a caregiver yourself, you could become like a sister or brother or even a parent to someone who is caregiving alone. As a friend or neighbor, you could *be there* for another so that he or she could continue the work without harming his or her own health.

The Role of Empathy in Determining Your Psychological Family

To reiterate, what caregivers need from their families is affection, caring, reassurance, advice, guidance, proximity, assistance, nurturance, reliable visits, and tangible help.[9] But what makes all this possible? Empathy.

From my view as a clinician, empathy is the capability to identify with and understand another person's feelings, beliefs, needs, and actions. It's the ability to walk in another's shoes and to experience what he or she is experiencing.

Can we learn empathy? Yes, but to do so, we need to let go of ego. We must let go of the need to focus on ourselves. Karen Armstrong writes of people getting along, of the need for us to develop "a habit of empathy."[10] This involves doing unto others as you would have them do unto you—traditionally known as the Golden Rule.

Nearly every religion in the world has a rule about giving back and helping others. For many, the Golden Rule means actually *doing* good deeds, deeds that you wish would be done for you in a similar circumstance. For others, the ethic is not about doing but about *restraint*—not harming others.

In the case of caregiving, the rule of doing, for example, means that we would actually help a caregiver, whereas the rule of restraint means, for example, curbing time at work so that we don't abandon a caregiver who is overwhelmed. Clearly, both ethics—doing and not doing—can lead to the same positive end for those who are distressed and suffering.

To practice the habit of empathy, we must acknowledge the immense service that family caregivers give to our society today, but we must also do more. As relatives, friends, neighbors, and community members, we must regularly lend a hand to help. Although Armstrong states that "looking after somebody else means that you have to give yourself away,"[11] she may be referring to ego, not to martyring or losing oneself in the process. Her point—and mine—is that we commit to helping others because we empathize with them and would wish for the same if we were in need.

In every neighborhood today, there's a lesson in empathy—or the lack of it. As a society, we need more empathy, not just for the ill and infirm, but also to preserve the health and dignity of people like you who are taking care of others, quietly and too often alone.

In 1967, Norman Paul, a psychiatric expert on loss and grief with whom I used to discuss ideas at family therapy conferences, wrote, "Each of us appears to have a basic hunger for empathy, a wish for the intimacy that can erase, if only for a moment, the individual's sense of emptiness and aloneness. Paradoxically, we want to satisfy this hunger, but, at the same time, we erect facades and barriers to prevent our being touched by real people."[12]

This could explain why both the book and the film version of *The Notebook* were so popular. The story is of two people who love each other to the end, despite the woman's dementia. Her memory revives now and then as her husband reads to her from the notebook she kept about their life together.

Perhaps the reason people love such stories is that they can empathize without risk. They know that their time with the characters is temporary—two hours or so for a film, a few more to read a book. In either case, the time needed for compassion is short. This, however, is just spectator empathy.

Paul believed that empathy was so vital to human well-being that we seek it even in our entertainment, especially in fiction and theater. Spectator empathy allows us to experience relatively little pain: we know the characters are fictional, that this is not our family, and that the show will be over soon. We won't have to commit any further to caring about these people. So Paul may have been right: we hunger to express empathy, but like to do it in venues where the story supplies the comfort of closure. There is no need then to offer affection, caring, reassurance, guidance, assistance, nurturance, visits, and tangible help. The story is over.

Loving a person with dementia in real life, however, has no clear ending, and that is our real challenge—to stay empathetic and connected in a real life story that remains ambiguous.

I confess I love a good tearjerker film or book, but now I see that although films and books about the pain of loving someone with dementia stimulate discussion and are educational, they are at best temporary solutions to our empathic urges. Better we should look down the street

84

or in our own families. There are some real people there who need our compassion and support.

■ ■

When someone you love has dementia, the players in your family may be reluctant and without empathy. Some may live far away and don't see the urgency of the situation. Others live nearer by, but assume that a designated family member will do the caring work. You may even apologize for them, saying the others are too busy with their own lives, so they can't help. Or that no one else can give care as well as you can. Relatives may be relieved by these rationalizations, but this attitude could lead to trouble. Just as dementia's loss is strange and confusing, so are the family relationships that follow. Whether families are biological or psychological, more empathy is needed all around.

If you don't have a family that can help you, I am giving you license to make one up. A neighbor becomes a grandparent or mother figure, a friend becomes a sister, a friend's father becomes a father figure, a therapist becomes a generic parent, and members of the clergy become spiritual advisers. Form a family of choice, one made up of like-minded people who give mutual support and help one another. Or if certain people were comforting to you in hard times while they were alive, then keep them in your heart and mind now. Remember what they said, and say it to yourself as if you are now their proxy. Imagined support can lower stress as much as actual support. Many people also keep a spiritual presence. They tell me that they walk with God and that feeling his presence is their ultimate comfort. And today we see millions of people connecting regularly via the Internet—chat rooms, blogs, and social networking sites. Groups of caregivers become like families.

Real, live, accessible people make up our psychological families, but so can those who are not physically available if they continue to exist in our hearts and minds.

Sam's Story

Sam was a smart, strong man, who came to me full of pain and despair. His wife, a once-successful teacher, was beginning to forget things and make bad decisions. She was no longer the woman he married, and now that the children were gone, he felt he deserved to have some easier times. Instead, life was getting harder. He had to take charge but didn't want to, nor did she trust him to do so.

"I feel like I'm in a vise," he said. "Life is an uphill climb now—just when I thought it would be getting easier. My wife is no longer there for me. She doesn't know what to do next, and she's like … gone. I feel alone. I'm so mad at her that I yell at her. Why can't she see what she's doing to me?"

After getting confirmation that his wife was indeed diagnosed with Alzheimer's disease, I asked Sam, "Might you be what I call a reluctant caregiver? Reluctant to give up the relationship you had? Reluctant to take on the workload? Reluctant to give up your job or leisure time?" But he wasn't ready to answer. I understood. It takes time to accept a caregiving role. No one is ready for it. "We are all reluctant caregivers," I said. In that moment, he seemed calm.

Yet Sam's contempt and anger were getting out of control and hurting both of them. Before he could find compassion, he needed to learn self-regulation and less rigid thinking. He was lonely, and thought it was all about him. "Why should I feel sorry for her?" he asked. "She should feel sorry for me!"

"Might it be that being angry is easier for you than grieving?" I asked.

"Yes, I suppose so," he said, "but I can't let go of the idea that she's just acting and could get better if she wanted to." Then he smiled and said quietly, "That's not realistic, is it?"

We talked about justice and how life is often unfair. "It's really unfair for you both, Sam, but that fact doesn't condone your yelling at her. That has to stop." We made a contract in which he promised to curb his anger while we worked on his sadness and grief for what he was losing—a competent, loving, and protective wife, as well as his own dreams of retirement. We talked about his strengthening himself emotionally. Rather than remaining angry about no longer being able to lean on his wife, he could take pride in being strong enough for her to lean on him. His compassion started to grow. Although he found it difficult to understand her feelings and to imagine what she was going through in losing her memory, with the help of his sister and some close friends—his psychological family—he was able to see his wife through their eyes. With their validation and steady support, his empathy grew.

Sam finally saw that his wife's behavior was unintentional and that it was the illness that robbed both of them. It took months of peer-group work and some therapy for him to see that her failures were neither her fault nor his. As his empathy grew, his anger subsided. His memories of his caring grandfather gave him a role model, and he thought of him often. Despite the extra work, he became more loving. His wife's anxiety lessened, and they worked out a "good-enough" relationship—not like the one they had, but one with sufficient connection to see movies together, dine with friends, and visit family for special events. (More will be said about the good-enough relationship in Chapter Nine.)

An important point: Sam was *not* settling or accepting his lot; rather, he was relinquishing ego and control and the belief that he could fix any problem if he tried hard enough. By shifting his way of thinking and reaching out to others for help and human connection, he regained control of himself and how he defined his situation.

And that brings us to the next chapter, on family rituals—the celebrations, traditions, and gatherings that are the glue of any kind of family life. They can provide support and continuity during times of stress and change—and thereby strengthen your resilience.

⫸ *Ideas for Reflection and Discussion* ⫷

WHO IS IN YOUR PSYCHOLOGICAL FAMILY?

Take out a blank sheet of paper and draw a large circle on it to represent the boundary of your family. Fill it in with stick figures, initials, or formal genogram symbols[13] to represent the people you think of as family.

* Who is in?

* Who is out?

* Whom do you want to have attend your most special occasions—birthdays, graduations, and weddings? Whom do you want to see on religious holidays or at your holiday table?

* Whom do you want to be with you in times of joy or sorrow?

* Whom do you trust to be there when you need help?

* Who is there for you when you need to express your thoughts or ask for help?

- Who has given you support?
- Who is fully present for you so that you don't have to feel alone?
- Who is cognitively and emotionally available to you?

We all need someone like family to be there for us—someone who can play the role when real family members cannot—when a parent is ill, when a sibling is far away, when sons and daughters have their own children to care for. To manage the work of caregiving, seek others who can fill the roles when your own family members cannot. Your own health depends on it.

6

Family Rituals, Celebrations, and Gatherings

[Family rituals] point to a direction for making sense of the
loss while enabling continuity for the living.

—EVAN IMBER-BLACK, *"RITUALS AND THE HEALING PROCESS,"*
IN LIVING BEYOND LOSS, 2004, p. 340

I t's no accident that I write this chapter while on
retreat at Saint John's University and Monastery
in Minnesota. Rituals and their symbols permeate
life here. Bells ring regularly to remind monks of prayer,
classes meet at regular times, people gather for mass,
and university students graduate at the end of each year
with elaborate ceremony. In the countryside surrounding
the campus, the rhythms of the seasons are ritualized
by planting and harvesting, as well as by the holidays its

91

people celebrate—Christmas or Hanukkah in winter, Easter or Passover in spring, Thanksgiving in late fall.

In this peaceful place, I ponder my questions about family rituals and how they can help people find meaning when a loved one has dementia. Taking a break, I walk from the Abbey Guesthouse, where I've been writing, to the next building to see the finished pages of the new Saint John's Bible—a unique project that merges the ancient arts of calligraphy and illumination with old as well as surprisingly new images. I was startled—and deeply moved—when I saw on one page, illustrated in gold leaf, the image of the World Trade Center in New York, the twin towers, as they were before 9/11. On another page, among ancient symbols of suffering, there were the strands of the DNA double helix of the AIDS virus. These contemporary symbols of suffering, combined with the traditional, are for me the most profound examples of change made in an instrument of ritual today.

If a family of Benedictines can update their sacred illustrations for the Bible, then our own families, regardless of faith, should be able to change and adapt our own rituals and celebrations when illness strikes. Yet even though there are many rituals and symbols to help us make sense of a death in the family, there are virtually none to help us mourn the loss of someone who is still alive.

A Primer on Family Rituals

To adapt or create new rituals to fit your situation now, you first need to know what rituals are, what purposes they serve, and how your family and community culture influence them.

What Are Family Rituals?

Family rituals are repeated interactions, traditions, and celebrations that give us a sense of closeness and belonging to a particular group.[1] *Patterned interactions* include family dinners, bedtime routines, and weekend activities. *Family traditions* include birthdays, anniversaries, and family reunions. *Family celebrations* include special occasions, such as weddings and religious holidays. As a group, these rituals are, of course, influenced by our culture and spiritual beliefs, and often are repeated across the generations.[2] Family rituals can range from elaborate religious celebrations to simple, repeated daily interactions, such as saying hello and good-bye when loved ones leave or return.[3] Although cultural anthropologists and family therapists were the first to identify the positive effects of family rituals,[4] researchers now confirm that "family rituals are powerful organizers of behaviors within the family system"[5] and are good for mental health.

93

Sometimes, of course, family rituals can be harmful. If, for example, an event always includes drinking, abusive language or behavior, or fighting, reach out to your psychological family and engage in healthier ways of celebrating. Family rituals can also be hurtful when they are unnecessarily rigid about including only some of the family—for example, when children are not allowed (presumably as a measure of emotional protection) to participate in a grandparent's birthday celebration because it now takes place in a nursing home, or when they are not permitted to attend funerals.

Who Benefits?

Family rituals have symbolic meaning for a particular group, so outsiders may not understand or benefit from them.[6] Like sports teams, fraternities and sororities, clubs, and religious orders, families possess the insider knowledge to understand what their individual rituals mean. Your ways of grieving and honoring the dead may not be the same as your neighbor's. And when you perform rituals to grieve the loss of your loved one while he or she is still here, outsiders may not understand. When you have no more tears left to shed at a funeral, when you have dinner with a friend once a week to curb your loneliness, outsiders may not understand. The people in your family circle, those who care about *you*, will realize that such rituals keep you connected and healthy.

94

How Many Should You Have?

Some families have a lot of rituals, others have none.[7] Aim for the middle ground.[8] Have at least a few—celebrate birthdays and major holidays. Don't allow dementia to interrupt the fun just when you need it most.

How Can Family Rituals Help You?

Although traditional family rituals are not designed to deal with the losses associated with dementia, they have the unique capacity to hold and symbolize contradictions—life and death, gain and loss, joy and sadness.[9] Traditional rituals celebrate new life or grieve a death, but they have to be newly crafted for an ambiguous loss. Here, sadness and joy are simultaneous, and both need to be acknowledged. Some kind of gathering helps you find meaning in the middle ground—having a loved one who is here but not here. If flexible, rituals can help you mark even an ambiguous loss, which religion and the larger society may not notice. This, of course, depends on your culture.

Until others acknowledge your losses, it may be hard for you to cope and grieve. To stay resilient, you can benefit from having some small rituals along the way to mark each new loss as it occurs to you. Perform these with at least one other person, because marking a loss in the presence of others makes it more real and yet more bearable.

Rituals give you a way to acknowledge the pain of loss and change while also providing you with the comfort of connection and continuity.[10]

From birth to death, rituals define not only your identity but also who your family is—who's in and who's out.[11] For caregivers, rituals reveal who's on your team—and thus who will be there for you when you need help and support. Gathering together, whether for Sunday brunch or a special holiday, provides a visible picture of solidarity—one that can lift you up and give you the motivation to keep going. Again, if your biological family is unavailable or is unable to participate, find a psychological family that can.

Overall, family rituals increase your social connection. In being with other people, you gain a sense of belonging and stability despite the instability of illness. When one relationship is impaired by dementia, your well-being depends on predictable and satisfying relationships with others.[12]

Finally—and this point may be controversial—some people believe that family rituals can help you settle your relationship "accounts." According to Ivan Böszörményi-Nagy and Geraldine Spark, family rituals "traditionally dealt with contractual obligations among people and between God and man."[13] Ancient rituals were meant to balance unsettled accounts through sacrifice and thanksgiving offerings. Burial ceremonies were meant to balance unsettled accounts between the dead and the living. Wedding ceremonies were a matter of business.

From this perspective, people who are taking care of a parent may be overly zealous as caregivers because they feel a need to repay their parents now for the care they received from them as a child. These are the caregivers who often wear themselves out.

I also see the opposite: caregivers who are reluctant because as children, they were neglected or abused by the parents who now need their care. Theirs is understandably a difficult challenge with no perfect solution. I often recommend in-home professional care, assisted living, or full-time care at a group residence so that the adult child doesn't have to do the hands-on care. Even though now and then there is a transformation of forgiveness, the goal for the most part is to find good care for the elder without judging the adult child.

Although I don't advocate balancing the ledger as *the* solution to relationship issues, numerous caregivers have told me that they feel the need to settle accounts, one way or the other, in order to eventually find peace.

Where Should Rituals Take Place?

Rituals traditionally take place in the home or in religious and sacred settings,[14] but family rituals for grieving the ambiguous loss of dementia can take place wherever you are—at home or at the seashore, on an island or in the mountains, in a concert hall or theater, in the countryside or a city park, or in a garden or chapel at a nursing home or hospital—anywhere that has meaning and symbolizes what you have lost. There is no right place for such rituals. Perform them wherever you can and with at least one other person. Play a song, read a poem, walk a familiar path, say a prayer, light a candle, send up a balloon, and so on. Talk with your family and friends for more ideas.

What Is the Right Time?

We are told that grief rituals across cultures are confined as to when and where they can take place.[15] This is not true with dementia; it has no time or location restrictions. The need for mourning rituals is continuous, like a book that has no end.

As I've mentioned, when working through chronic grief, you need rituals along the way to mark each loss as it happens. Do not wait for an approved time to grieve. Do it when you notice each loss—when your loved one is no longer able to travel, when he or she no longer knows who you are, when he or she loses continence or the ability to eat, and so on. Have a friend or family member with you, because the crux of rituals is to provide human connection.

The Reverend Robin Raudabaugh once told me, "Creating meaningful rituals is not only important but also necessary for our spiritual lives to mark thresholds and important points in our lives. They are for times of beginning and moving on—and actually, anything on which we place importance." In this context, a more flexible view of rituals strongly applies. Neither time nor place is rigidly set; it's your choice.

How Does Culture Influence Family Rituals?

Culture creates our systems of meaning,[16] so it also shapes our rituals and celebrations. But what if our culture is one that denies loss, and favors certainty over ambiguity? In this case, the dominant meaning system works against our particular situation—living with dementia.

Cultures also have meaning systems that help us understand our suffering. "Fatalistic cultures believe that traumatic events have external causes that must be continually faced during life; causes and consequences do not disappear."[17] Rituals and symbolic places are therefore needed to rehabilitate and support people during troubled times. In contrast, our more mastery-oriented culture is prone to blame the victim. Those who can't find solutions are assumed to be unsuccessful. What is important to recognize is that until there's a cure for dementia, families must endure the stress and pain of ambiguous loss. It isn't their fault. Staying connected through rituals and celebrations shows support rather than reproach.

What Not to Do

Family rituals are, for the most part, helpful for caregivers, especially if families can be flexible. However, they can also be the source of great distress. Here are some examples of what *not* to do.

Don't Cancel Christmas

When a loved one has dementia, families may be in a bind. They don't want to change their usual rituals and celebrations, but these rituals and celebrations may no longer work for everyone anymore. To avoid change, some families cancel the event altogether. This is saying that the happy times are gone if the gatherings can't be the way they always were. Change may also mean that relationships will never again be the same. Some people think in absolute terms; they give up, close the door, and act as if the good times are gone forever. Life after loss doesn't have to be this way.

These situations are prime for both-and thinking. Both-and thinking allows you to see possibilities for both change *and* continued good times. A graduation party is adapted and moved to a more accessible building. A wedding is moved to a hospital chapel so that the parent with dementia can be there. Thanksgiving dinner turns into a potluck and moves to wherever caregiver and patient can be easily included. Birthday parties are simplified and take place at a location with wheelchair accessibility.

100

Family vacations take place nearer to home, perhaps sometimes even in the backyard so that help is available when needed. Relatives who live far away spend a week of their annual vacations in the home of the patient so that the regular caregiver can get away. As in a relay, family members from afar come back home to help, one relieving the other, and then back around again. Holidays and birthdays need not be celebrated on their actual dates. Flexibility is key because without it, families fall apart.

Don't Expect the Women to Do It All

As we've established, women do most of the caregiving—but, in addition, they are also expected to be the keepers of family rituals—the dinners, the gifts, the reunions. Unless others in the family step up to help or take over, overburdened caregivers often opt out. Disagreements may follow. Researchers have found that family holidays and celebrations are the most difficult unresolved issues in the marital relationship of couples with aging parents.[18] They also have found that women were the most distressed. To enlist others in the family to take some responsibility for family gatherings, a session or two with a family therapist will help.

Don't Fight with Family

Families also cancel rituals and celebrations because they fear hurtful fights, which often escalate when dealing with

101

a person who has dementia. If conflict over care issues can't be resolved through rational discussion,[19] I again recommend family therapy. Good communication and teamwork can be learned.

Don't Submit to Stigma

Families often cancel their rituals and gatherings because of the social stigma that still exists around dementia. This stigma causes embarrassment and shame, which makes some caregivers reluctant to take their charges out in public. In a culture that denies death, we have to work harder to counteract the stigma against dementia. Notice those caregivers and families who carry on proudly in public social gatherings that include the patient. They simply ignore those who stigmatize and judge. Take a lesson from the Native Americans who tell me they are honored when elders with dementia join them in public ceremonies.

No one has to be perfect. Don't be embarrassed. Ignore those who criticize. In fact, become an advocate for accessibility everywhere in your community—and go out often.

Don't Continue When It's Dangerous

Deborah and her husband loved their yearly ritual of travel to distant places. Even though he had been diagnosed with Lewy body disease, a particularly ravaging kind of dementia that causes hallucinations, she continued the ritual of an annual trip. This year it was to be Alaska, and they were to go with friends, but at the last minute, the other couple had an emergency and couldn't go. What to do now?

> I had a feeling this might be our last trip, so I wanted to go. It was wonderful for me in some ways—to be on the ferry in that beautiful place—but at the same time, he was paranoid and wanted to be with me all the time. I felt claustrophobic, so I said, "I'm going up on the deck to read my book." "Well, can't I come?" he asked. I said I needed to be alone for a bit. When I came back, he accused me of having affairs. It was crazy paranoia. I felt guilty, so I tried hard to reassure him, but it wasn't working. He continued the questioning. "Where did you go? To some goddamn beauty pageant?" It was getting so crazy, but I didn't cry. Not yet. I was just stunned. There was no escape from it. Seeing Alaska was wonderful, but I was on alert all the time, afraid of what would come next. I got a black eye one night when he had night terrors. "What happened to our nice life?" he asked in a moment of lucidity. I couldn't do anything about it at first—it was too hard for me to admit it. Finally, I did.

Success comes with being resilient and flexible. Being able to continue celebrations and rituals requires people to change both during the caregiving journey as well as after it's over.

In order to restore safety, Deborah knew that their tradition of traveling to far-off places together had to change. She and her husband continued the tradition of annual trips, but now only as far as a nearby cabin on a lake, where family and friends could be around. "That worked," she said. Now, years later after her husband died, Deborah is traveling longer distances again, alone or with friends, and is gradually balancing the immensity of her loss with some new experiences and connections. Her resiliency served her well then—and now.

Success Stories

Many people seamlessly adapt their usual rituals when the person who ordinarily prepared them now has dementia. The shifting of roles and tasks can be a smooth family dance in which the elderly parent now sits on the sidelines—still there, but no longer in charge. Although not all generational shifts go smoothly, there are successes, as illustrated in a friend's story:

> Our family has had to revise our Christmas celebration since my Mom's stroke and resulting dementia. My sister makes the chocolate sauce (using Mom's recipe) for the ice cream my mom always made, my brother provides the holiday

nuts Mom always brought, I buy the gifts for the grandchildren so Mom has something to hand to them. We, as a family, are letting go of Mom's participation in the holiday, but at the same time, we're holding onto traditions that are important to us. It also gives me hope that our traditions will continue after Mom is no longer with us—part of my "imagining new hope."

If people are willing to be flexible and to accept some changes to accommodate illness, as Deborah and my friend and her siblings did, dementia shouldn't cheat you out of the good times. Family rituals and celebrations provide a sense of continuity and predictability, which in turn increases your sense of belonging and stability. Whether your family is biological or psychological, continue getting together. It's important that you not feel alone on this long and difficult journey.

⚜ *Ideas for Reflection and Discussion* ⚜

❋ Family rituals include family dinners, bedtime routines, and weekend leisure activities; birthdays, anniversaries, and family reunions; and celebrations such as weddings and religious holidays.[20] They can be elaborate or simple, but they should involve at least one other person.

- Although there are no specific rituals for grieving ambiguous losses such as dementia, creating some way of marking the loss and honoring your loved one makes your loss real and allows others to acknowledge it.
- Family rituals can be detrimental if they involve harmful activities or are too rigid in who can or cannot attend or participate.
- Find people who will help you brainstorm new rituals—other caregivers or close friends—people who are empathic and understand what you are going through. These may be part of your psychological family.
- For caregivers, family rituals show you who's on your team and who's there for you when you need help or support.
- A caregiver's need for grief rituals is continuous because the losses from dementia are continuous.
- Consider your culture, religious beliefs, and personal values. What fits your values and beliefs about how to grieve for a loved one who is still here?
- Mark each loss with a flower, candle, song, poem, a balloon sent into the air, a paper crane

sent out to sea, or a planting in your garden. Do something that symbolizes your particular loss.

✲ Which rituals have eased your stress? Have any excluded you or been canceled?

✲ Think about the roles you perform in family rituals and celebrations. Are they too rigid? Can your family update them to be more flexible?

✲ List what would make your participation (and your loved one's) more feasible. Tell a family member what changes are needed.

✲ Find someone with whom you can have a routine of meeting daily or, at minimum, weekly, to share a meal, go for a walk, or just chat.

7

Seven Guidelines for the Journey

There is only one way: Go within.

—RAINER MARIA RILKE, LETTERS TO A YOUNG POET, *1929/2000, p. 11*

If you are to function, your journey as a caregiver requires you to hold two opposing ideas at the same time—in this case, caring for yourself and caring for another. This requires self-reflection.

Caring for someone you love means that you have to accept imperfect solutions: allowing someone else to do the caring work while you take a bit of time off, sharing your role, and perhaps, moving your loved one to institutional care. Finding the middle ground is painful, but the alternative is dangerous. The question of how to be a good caregiver has multiple answers, but taking care of yourself is always one of them.

The ways that caregivers take care of themselves reflect cultural differences in attitudes, beliefs, norms, and values. Religion, socioeconomic status, geographical regions, gender, race, and age all influence the meaning and attitudes you have about caregiving.[1] What we know so far is that the early stages of the disease (even before diagnosis) are very stressful for caregivers[2] and that severe and long-term chronic stress is not good for caregivers' health.[3]

What may surprise you most, however, is that your stress affects the person you care for as well. That is, the more distressed you are, the more distressed and behaviorally unpredictable the person with dementia will be.[4] This fact may be the best motivator for you to take care of yourself.

To do this, I now ask you to focus on yourself and your own experience. Reflect on the following ideas about meaning, mastery, identity, ambivalence, attachment, and hope. Ponder these ideas alone, and also discuss them with others in a discussion group, a support group, a book club, or on a blog. (Information to help with such groups can be found in the Resources section at the back of this book.) You can also discuss these ideas with a professional.

Know that these are guidelines, not a to-do list of items that must be accomplished in a specific order or by specific times. There is neither the comfort nor the pressure of a clear deadline. In living with dementia and its ambiguous loss, a more flexible set of guidelines works better.

Therefore, there is no rigid sequence to the following seven guidelines, nor must you give each the same degree of attention. Tailor them to your own needs. Your goal is not perfection, but rather doing the best you can to take care of yourself on a journey that is long and stressful.

Guideline One: Find Meaning

To find meaning means being able to understand your experience. But in the case of dementia, meaning is especially hard to find because of its ambiguous nature. When your loved one is here but not here, and that incongruity persists, it's difficult to make sense of your relationship. Everything you thought you had a grasp on is now confusing.

Despite this confusion, finding meaning is essential if you are to avoid feeling helpless and hopeless. How can you find meaning in this such uncanny loss? By accepting two ideas simultaneously: your relationship is strangely lost—yet it still exists.

To comfortably accept dual thinking, consider your beliefs. If you believe that a loved one's presence has to be absolute, if you assume that people are either absent or present and that they can't be both, then such thinking may not work for you. Yet I urge you to give it a try. It's a useful way to find meaning when the person you love has dementia. You can live with contradictions once you acknowledge the reality of them in your life.

111

Finding meaning therefore takes time. Often it emerges in narrative form—through the writing or telling of one's own story. Christopher Buckley, the son of William F. Buckley, is one of seventy-seven million baby boomers now trying to make sense of their caregiving experience with elderly parents. In *Losing Mum and Pup*, Buckley poignantly describes what he felt about "the awful daily lot" of seeing both of his formerly independent parents become so utterly dependent on him:

> He was clutching my arm. It wrenched my heart.
> This was terra nova to me: the delusional parent
> who must be denied for his own good. Every fiber
> of one's being reflexively inclines to accede to the
> wishes of a parent. It is *contra naturam* ... to say
> no to someone who has raised you, clothed you,
> fed you from day one—well, even if, in Pup's case,
> these actual duties were elaborately subcontracted;
> still, it feels as though you're disobeying and
> in contravention of the Fourth Commandment
> [that one must honor one's father and mother].
> This is the crushing, awful daily lot of the
> children of Alzheimer's patients. "No, Mom,
> let's *not* put our fingers in the blender, okay?"[5]

How does a good son or daughter make sense of tending once competent parents? Buckley looked up to his famous parents—they insisted on it—and now they were totally dependent on him.

I share this story with you because we may forget that caregiving hits people from many walks of life. It is difficult for everyone. It takes a while to find some meaning in the stressful paradox—that of the child now parenting the parent.

Mary, too, was distressed, but her struggle was to make sense of the relationship with her once brilliant husband, now diagnosed with dementia. "It doesn't really matter what it's called though; he's just not himself anymore. I just don't know what to do."

Mary's husband had been an extremely successful doctor and now was unable to load the dishwasher. He had always been friendly and helpful to her and to others, but he became sullen and withdrawn. "I miss him," she said. "My family made me take a caregiver test, and now on top of his illness, they tell me I have depression." She was devastated over her diagnosis.

From my observation of Mary—with her vast network of friends, her family and social support network, her energy, her continued optimism and sense of humor, I wasn't so sure that she was depressed. I was sure, however, that she was sad and grieving.

"I don't think you're depressed," I said, "but you are sad, and you have a right to be." Mary sighed with relief.

"You're losing your wonderful husband day by day, and day by day, you're grieving that loss. That's normal."

To Mary, the diagnosis of depression meant a deficiency on her part, but being told she was sad and grieving meant she was normal. It made sense to her and made her feel more able to withstand what was to come. With validation, she could think dualistically. "I hate what it has done to him and to my life, but my life is still much, much better than most in this situation. I delight in what we can do, and take great joy and comfort in the support and help of many wonderful people who bring understanding and compassion for this long journey."

Even after Mary acknowledged her sadness and anger, she showed resiliency in her story—becoming comfortable with discussing the good and the bad. She was able to understand both sides of her situation.

Not everyone attributes the same meaning to a diagnosis of depression as Mary did, but many caregivers tell me they dislike being labeled "sick." When they are diagnosed with depression, they often feel embarrassed. To them, it means they have failed, as though they'll no longer be able to care as well for their loved one.

■ ■

I am always surprised by how differently people find meaning. In one caregiver group, I was explaining some new research about grief.[6] As I discussed in Chapter Two, grief is an oscillating process, never finished completely, but with ups and downs of sadness wider apart over time—with perhaps closer oscillations again upon anniversaries of the loss or when life transitions would have taken place and now cannot.

While I was explaining this oscillation to the caregiver group, a man in the back spoke up: "I'm an engineer,"

114

he said, "and I'm learning things here today I didn't learn in engineering. But it makes sense—the idea of oscillation—and it helps me understand what I am going through."

For him, meaning was found through the language of engineering. Others find understanding through poetry and music. And still others do so through religious stories—such as the story of Job, who eventually regained happiness despite immense loss. No matter how you find meaning in your loss, patience is vital.

Guideline Two: Balance Control with Acceptance

In a culture that values mastery and problem solving, accepting ambiguity implies failure. People want their lives to be manageable. When there's no certainty about how long a person with dementia can live, you may be tempted to shift to absolute thinking—considering your loved one already gone from your life or denying that anything is wrong. But absolute responses are a fabrication and thus create even more stress—brittleness, not resiliency. Better we learn to tolerate ambiguity and to have faith that things will turn out even if, in the present moment, we can't understand how.

When we can't control what's going on around us, we can still master our thoughts, reactions, and internal selves. Such spiritual strength comes in many ways:

through prayer, meditation, music, poetry, and other creative expressions. Others find inner control by mastering their bodies athletically, their minds intellectually—and both with mindfulness. But Helen, the longtime caregiver I referred to in Chapter Three, who put bad news in her pocket until she could handle it, found yet another way to stay in charge. She used what I call "functional denial"—sometimes a useful method of coping.

When Helen was given the news about the seriousness of her loved one's dementia, the doctor thought she wasn't listening and told her so. She was offended. Her temporary denial was a conscious action. She knew what she was doing. Creatively, she found a way to hold on to some control in one place while she was losing it in another.

No matter how hard we work or how good we are, the world doesn't always go our way. Bad things do happen to good people.[7] Dementia is one of those bad things. How can you maintain some control? Recall the Serenity Prayer, one version of which is "God, give us grace to accept with serenity the things that cannot be changed, courage to change the things that should be changed, and the wisdom to distinguish the one from the other."[8]

To stay in control, differentiate what you can control from what you cannot. When you've tried everything, and there's nothing else you can do, go with the flow.

Embrace the ambiguity. Know that the world isn't always fair—that things don't always go your way and that this isn't your fault. You're doing the best you can.

Depending on what you are accustomed to, adjust your need for control either down *or* up. Some people need to tighten the reins, others to loosen them. The goal is to know *when* to increase or lower your need to manage things. There are times when we ought to ramp up our effort to master a problem, and others when we would do better to ramp down our need for mastery. Over this, we do have control.

It is useful to know that the more you seek mastery and control, the more distressed you may be when losses remain ambiguous, as they do with dementia. To lower your stress, find something you *can* control, no matter how small. How about dinner with a friend on a *fixed* night each week or watching a TV program *undisturbed*? Or having a helper come in to relieve you at a *predictable* time each day or week? Simplify outings, celebrations, rituals, and gatherings. Call a family meeting and insist on help so that your life is not always controlled by dementia.

In a culture of mastery, we need something we can control in order to balance what we cannot. If we don't, we feel dangerously hopeless. Might it be that we are terrorized by ambiguity even more than by death? (More will be said about this in Chapter Eight.)

Guideline Three: Broaden Your Identity

Who are you, now that dementia has entered your relationship? Are you still someone's child if your parent can't remember your name? Are you still married if your spouse no longer knows you? Who is your family now?

When we can't clarify whether a loved one is in or out of our lives, our identity becomes confused. The husband whose wife no longer knows him wonders if he's still married; he doesn't feel that he is. The daughter of a mother with dementia wonders if she is still a daughter or if she is now her mother's parent. Confusion reigns. Without concrete verification of loss, one's status and roles slide into limbo, causing anxiety and depression in even the strongest persons. The goal is to revise your identity to fit the ambiguity. Certainly not an easy task, but it can be done.

Maria did it. She saw herself now as her mother's caregiver, but occasionally her mother would reclaim her role: "Remember, I'm still your mother!" Maria would acquiesce with a smile on her face. Humor got her through. She knew she was in charge, but she'd let her mother's protests pass because she knew they were temporary—and they reminded Maria of her former identity as someone's daughter. They brought back good memories—and always a smile.

Here again, both-and thinking helps you reconstruct your identity. You're both child *and* parent to a parent.

You may feel both married *and* not married. Hanging on to one absolute identity when your loved one has dementia only increases your stress.

Reconstruct the roles you play. As a wife, you may now be the head of the family, provider, money manager, and chauffeur, along with your usual roles. As a husband, you may now be nurturer, cook, housekeeper, plus all you were before. What was considered men's or women's work before is now the work of the healthier person, whoever that is. It should not, however, be delegated only to the women in a family.

Ask yourself these questions: Who is allowed to do what in my family? Is there a team approach, or am I expected to do all the work alone? What are my family's unofficial rules based on race, religion, class, age, or gender? For example, is there an unspoken rule in my family that only women and girls can be caregivers? Are certain people excused from helping? Why? Can my family talk about change?

Become aware of the rules and question them. There often needs to be a new rule about teamwork so that caregiving doesn't fall on one person's shoulders. Include men and boys as well as girls and women in these discussions. Think about how you see yourself now. Besides being a caregiver, who are you?

Ask yourself these questions: Is it right for me to go out with friends when a loved one has dementia? Do I still feel like a son or daughter? A spouse? A sibling? How should I act? Who should I be?

Each person's answers will be different, but the goal is to do what lowers your stress. Become more flexible. If family and social expectations influence your identity (and they often do), you don't have to abide. Knowing how dangerous caregiving is to your health, take a chance and do something that would be relaxing and fun; remember, it is important to take care of *you*.

Before we move on, there are a few more points to consider when reconstructing your identity. First, if your family or community stigmatizes dementia, reject this idea; it is born of ignorance. Dementia is not contagious, nor is it anyone's fault. Second, if your family or community believes that only females should be caregivers, reject this idea as too rigid and unfair. When women provide income in addition to taking care of the young, disabled, sick, and dying, they are overburdened and vulnerable to illness and premature death. Men and boys must help as well. Third, if your family or community believes that children and youth should not visit people with dementia, then both patient and caregiver become untouchables. Avoid this identity at all costs.

Guideline Four: Manage Your Mixed Emotions

Mixed emotions or ambivalent feelings are typical when you love someone who has dementia. If these feelings are unrecognized, the negative emotions in particular can emerge suddenly as anger or, worse yet, abuse. That's not acceptable. Mixed emotions are normal, but acting on them is not.

When you care for a loved one with dementia, it's normal to *feel* anger and guilt, and even wish for it all to be over, but it's imperative to talk with peers or professionals about such wishes for it all to end. Doing so prevents trouble. Feeling anger is understandable, but hurting yourself or the person you care for is unacceptable. Talk openly with a therapist or peers about your worst feelings. You may be surprised how many others have similar feelings now and then toward the person they care for. Wishing "it" were over is typical, but the challenge is to acknowledge and then manage such ambivalence.

Sarah's mother has dementia, and Sarah came to see me because she was deeply distressed. "There are times when I wish it were over—that she would die. Is this normal? I feel guilty when I think this way. But Mom is no longer aware of life. Am I wishing it for my sake or for hers? I don't know. All I know is that I feel guilty a lot of the time now."

These feelings are typical. What did I say to her? "First, it's normal to wish for someone's death if he or she is suffering. My question to you, Sarah, is this: Do you know if your mother is in pain or suffering in any way? Can you find this out from her physician?" That brought us to the second question: "Are you wishing for it to be over for your own sake because *you* are suffering?"

As Sarah's reaction implied, the answer to the last question was "Yes." I told Sarah that this was often the case. "We suffer immeasurably when someone we love appears to be suffering. Their pain is our pain. But it's up to us to manage our own pain."

Although some of us have been fortunate enough to have experienced less of it, suffering is a part of life—and inevitable when you love another person. Whenever suffering comes, we need resiliency enough to withstand the pain of loss. To think that one doesn't have to suffer is "ego wanting its own way."[9] With dementia, the big learning is that things *won't* go our way.

Guideline Five: Hold On *and* Let Go

With dementia, the attachment you had to your loved one may still be there, but now there is a categorical difference in your relationship.[10] Due to the dementia, the relationship is more one-sided than it used to be. Connection as you knew it has become increasingly difficult. With closure impossible, shift your perceptions of attachment to one of both-and: my loved one is *both* here *and* gone.

Revising attachment means taking the middle ground. You don't consider your relationship broken, nor do you deny that it's less secure. In this middle ground, ask yourself frequently, "How might my loved one want me to think or act on this or that?" Keeping him or her in your psychological family is helpful and may at times be all you have for comfort and guidance.

Through no fault of your own or the patient's, your secure attachment is now filled with anxiety. Yes, an anxious attachment. In slow motion, your loved one is disappearing, and you are being left behind. To confuse matters more, there are sometimes brief returns to normal, so that you become hopeful again, or else feel guilty that you had given up. Caregivers tell me they love these brief moments of reconnection, but such precious times also add to their anxiety and stress.

A friend once told me that sometimes she feels guilty because she can't always feel the same level of love as she once had for her mother. Although attachment is often ruptured by dementia, we still have choices. We can close that person out of our lives as if he or she were already gone—or we can settle for a partial relationship, one that is less than perfect. The latter is the better choice, but it requires a deeper humanity.

Accepting a partial relationship means that you continue to visit, talk to, and care for the person with dementia. You know that the compromised attachment results from illness and is not the fault of the patient, or you. Such close relationships are of course painful, so while you attend to them, you must also develop more secure attachments with others—friends and relatives who can be more fully present with you. One balances the deficits in the other.

Some clients tell me that they feel guilty meeting new friends or peers. Guilt may be inevitable, but you can learn to manage it, because the anxiety of developing new friends is less debilitating than the depression you will experience if you isolate yourself.

Guideline Six: Imagine New Hopes and Dreams

To stay strong, everyone needs hope, but you need a good imagination to find it in the midst of dementia. Brainstorm with other people who walk in your shoes and can empathize. Talk with young family members who often are less inhibited and more imaginative. It's important that while you give care, you also picture in your mind what your future might be like—with new connections, new hobbies, new travel plans, new skills, and new relationships.

Hope also comes from making peace with the ambiguity that surrounds your life. You may experience

124

a deepening of spirituality as you increase your tolerance for the unanswered questions. You trust more in what is unknown and temper your need for certainty. This opens up new options. You can laugh more easily at absurdity; you become less controlling and more patient.

Throughout the journey to find new hope, experience spirituality in your own way, whether through religion, nature, physical activity, sports, or the arts, including music, theater, paintings, and poetry. It is in community with others that you are most likely to find something to help you find new hopes and dreams.[11]

Perhaps your losses from dementia will never make sense to you, but knowing that some losses are incomprehensible—and always will be—is a meaning in itself and actually helps you move toward change and hope. Why? Because understanding that some losses are utterly senseless—and always will be—gives you the permission and freedom to let go of trying to find an absolute and perfect solution.

You begin to accept the paradox: you find meaning even in meaninglessness—and hope even in hopelessness.

Guideline Seven: Take the Time to Mind Yourself

In many airports (and I'm thinking particularly of one in Amsterdam), there are moving walkways that repeat and repeat in a melodic voice, "Mind your step! Mind your step! Mind your step!" as you reach the end. I thought of

125

this almost hypnotic warning when I was told that care-givers would roll their eyes if they read anything about taking care of themselves. "If you write this, they won't read it," I was told. Okay, I get it. It's just one more thing you have to worry about in an already overloaded day.

The responsibility for your health is more than yours alone. When you need help, lean on your friends, neighbors, relatives, your faith community, a recreational group, or a peer group of other caregivers led by experts who provide the information you need. Although everyone supports caregivers in theory, the reality is that most of us need to do more. We need to notice the difficult work you do and, at the very least, respond when you ask for help—or better yet, offer to help even before we're asked.

Doing good work without anyone knowing you are doing it is indeed praiseworthy, but your community needs to be made aware if it is to be educated and to change. As Barbara Pym writes in her novel *Excellent Women*, people ordinarily don't "do good by stealth."[12] Yet caregivers do. They are excellent women and men who constantly "do good by stealth" because no one but dementia patients witnesses the work they do. And patients can't often tell others about the good you do.

We should pay more attention to the necessary and isolating work done by so many people today. Whether the care you give is hands-on or long distance, I honor and value what you do. But I don't want you to compromise your own health.

Balancing Acts

Being a caregiver while also taking care of yourself can be a difficult balancing act. How do some caregivers do this? Julie couldn't get out of the house very often, so she used the Internet to connect with others while she was caring for her husband. In addition to communicating with friends and other caregivers, she also investigated colleges in her area where someday she might finish her degree. This focus on the future helped, she said, to keep her going while she was homebound. After her husband died, Julie did go back to school. It was something she had always wanted to do, and it gave her purpose—and a job—both of which she needed when she was no longer a caregiver.

Jan took care of herself by keeping up her social connections while also visiting her mate, Bob, as often as she could—not daily, but several times a week. Birthdays and holidays were celebrated at the home where he lived, with family and friends helping by organizing potlucks. Everyone enjoyed these gatherings, and no one was exhausted with preparations or transporting.

In other examples of self-care, Don follows his doctor's orders and goes to the gym twice a week; Laura goes to a monthly bingo night with friends at a nearby casino; Fred has a friend with whom he has dinner once a week; Jenna decided to keep her job but to step down to part-time, and says it's a relief to get out of the house a few hours each day; and Tim bought a computer, learned to surf the Internet, and joined a caring group he interacts with daily. "It's like having a friend right there beside you," he said.

While caring for someone you love, do him or her a favor. Take time to catch your breath. Stop trying to be perfect. Stop feeling guilty. Stop trying to control what can't be controlled. Find a way to get a good night's sleep.

Minding yourself is *not* selfish. Do it for the person you love who now needs you to stay healthy and strong. Tell your other family members that they have to pitch in more because if you no longer can, they will be the next in line. In essence, you're doing everyone—patient, family, and your community—a favor by taking time off.

There are times, however, when your life as a caregiver is so distressing that professional help is needed. Here are checklists to assess your own need.

Use the following checklists to assess how you're doing. Do this often, and discuss your assessment with your group leader or your physician. As you can see, the need to seek professional help is more urgent as you proceed farther down the lists.

Discuss with other caregivers or a professional if you feel

○ Sad as if grieving, mildly depressed but still functioning
○ Stuck or confused
○ Guilty about a decision you have to make
○ Feeling helpless about the procedures you are expected to perform
○ Unable to ask for help from other family members
○ No one is hearing you

See a licensed family therapist or relationship therapist if your

○ Family stress levels are so high that you are "walking on eggshells" and tense all the time
○ Relationships with spouse, children, and friends are put on hold because caregiving takes all your time
○ Conflict with family members, neighbors, and friends has increased
○ Family celebrations and rituals are cancelled, so there is no more family interaction
○ Family meetings to discuss the present situation are nonexistent or cancelled, and you feel abandoned as a caregiver
○ Relatives neglect both you and the patient, no one calls or offers to help, and there are no caregiver groups nearby

○ Adult children or stepchildren criticize but never help

○ Financial needs increase, but other family members never help or acknowledge the financial sacrifices you are making; in this case, you may also need to seek legal or financial advice

Sometimes, however, you need more. The following feelings are *not* typical. Seek immediate professional help if you

○ Feel so depressed or hopeless that you can't function

○ Feel so anxious you can't function

○ Feel physically ill

○ Feel in danger, having been hit or choked by the person you care for

○ Feel like hurting yourself

○ Feel like hurting or yelling at the person you care for

○ Depend too heavily on alcohol or recreational drugs

○ No longer take your prescribed medications or misuse them

○ No longer eat or sleep well

○ No longer care about taking care of yourself

○ See your own death as the only way out

If any one item on this last list applies to you, see a licensed professional—a psychologist, psychiatrist, social worker, family therapist, physician, or pastoral counselor—as soon as possible. Be honest. Tell him or her how you feel, for if you are disabled or die, the person you care for will no longer have the benefit of your care.

If none of these lists apply to you now, do as Anna did. She told me, "I like these lists to check myself against, maybe because none of them apply to me right now. But I'll keep checking." Good for you, Anna. Keep checking.

I've found that providing such tools as these checklists to "mind oneself" can be more effective than constantly telling caregivers to take care of themselves. Anna tells us why. "I resent people asking me the proverbial question: 'Are you taking care of yourself?' People have no idea what that really means. They have some grandiose idea of what taking care of myself means. What I see as taking care of myself is frequent, comfortable outings with supportive friends. They don't."

It's unfortunate that others saw Anna's self-care choice as frivolous. What they saw as their concern for her well-being, she saw as inauthenticity and lack of empathy. What's a caregiver to do? My recommendations: find people to be with who support you; minimize contact with those who don't; and don't feel guilty.

Relatives, neighbors, friends—and professionals— aren't always listening. They mean well, but are often less than genuine in hearing what caregivers say they need. Caregivers—the ones in my office, down the street, in our congregation, or in our own families—need more empathy. Ask them what would help, and don't be so quick to judge—for you could be walking in their shoes anytime.

131

It happens sometimes that a person—perhaps a family member or friend—is not cut out to do the work of caregiving. People who are short-tempered or insistent on being in control (or both) may not be able to adapt. They want to help, but wisely show reluctance. I respect such hesitancy and advise helping in other ways. Rather than having them provide hands-on caregiving, a better project might be doing the paperwork, contributing money toward hands-on care, or offering short-term respite for the full-time caregiver.

If you aren't a caregiver, you can still help. How about making a firm date for dinner with a caregiver? How about visiting a caregiver's house and playing a card game or board game, one that has a clear win-or-lose outcome? In the midst of ambiguity, clarity is soothing, no matter how trivial.

■ ■

Above all if you are a caregiver, don't take this journey alone. Find someone who is facing a similar loss. Each of your situations will vary based on the stage and depth of dementia, but you'll find some common ground. Take away ideas that are useful to you—that help you find the resiliency both to care for your loved one and to maintain your own health.

Think of it this way: caregiving for someone with dementia is like walking in the fog. It confuses you and makes you feel helpless and even hopeless at times. But you continue to move forward even though you don't know what the next step will bring. You mind your step so that you won't trip and fall. When you're exhausted, you take a break and get some rest. You call for help if you're stuck. This is taking care of yourself.

Ideas for Reflection and Discussion

These guidelines are adapted from my book *Loss, Trauma, and Resilience* (2006).

1. **Find Meaning**
   - The search for meaning is difficult when a loss is ambiguous and unclear.
   - The capacity to make sense of dementia requires both-and thinking. Sheer self-reliance is not enough; work on changing your way of thinking.
   - Shifting from a negative to a positive meaning can lower your stress.
   - Finding meaning must include some hope for your future.
   - Just as there is meaning in caring for people who are suffering from dementia, it also makes sense to take care of those who give the care.

2. **Balance Control with Acceptance**
   - Deciding to accept a situation is not the same as passively surrendering to it.
   - Know that the world isn't always fair and that what you're experiencing is not your fault.
   - Waiting passively for things to get better instead of actively coping will lead to depression. If you need help, see a licensed therapist who works with caregivers.
3. **Broaden Your Identity**
   - Know who you are and how your identity and roles have changed since you've become a caregiver.
   - See yourself as more than a caregiver; hanging on to one rigidly fixed identity is harmful.
   - Stay socially connected to prevent isolation and disconnection.
4. **Manage Your Mixed Emotions**
   - Understand that mixed emotions—love and hate, joy and anger—are typical, but they must be managed.
   - Talk about the bad feelings with someone professionally or in a group so that you don't act on them unconsciously.

✿ Talk about your guilt and shame with others so that you know that you are not alone.

✿ Take an anger management class, get treatment for addiction if that is a problem, learn money management if needed, learn to problem-solve where needed.

✿ Remember, ambiguous loss leads to ambivalence—but you can learn to manage it.

5. **Hold On *and* Let Go**

✿ Continue to touch, talk to, and visit with the person who has dementia.

✿ Go out and even take a vacation. It is not disloyal to the person you're caring for. She or he will benefit from your taking some time off.

✿ Make some new friends.

6. **Imagine New Hopes and Dreams**

✿ Let your former hopes and dreams give way to the discovery of new ones.

✿ Hope can hinder if it's unrealistic; imagine new options for change.

✿ Hope is not willed; it emerges from an excitement about being able to reach a larger goal.

135

7. Take the Time to Mind Yourself

✻ In addition to relationship issues, there are personal feelings, some of which are typical and some of which are life threatening.

✻ If you feel hopeless and so depressed that you no longer go out, seek help from your physician or a licensed professional who is experienced in working with caregivers and their families.

✻ If you feel sad and lonely, try to find a group that offers social support and stress management information. (Or see your primary doctor or a therapist for help.)

✻ If you are mildly depressed or sad, you may or may not need medication. Researchers are as yet unsure about medicating mild depression, but in any case, even mild depression must be attended to.[13] Join a group, gather information, listen to others tell their stories so you can learn how to cope. Information is power. Being with other people is uplifting.

✻ If you feel guilty asking for uninterrupted sleep, know that primary care physicians often help caregivers tell other family members how urgent this is and that they, as doctors, are asking for it, not you.

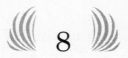

8

Delicious Ambiguity

"Hope" is the thing with feathers
That perches on the soul,
And sings the tune without the words,
And never stops—at all[.]

—EMILY DICKINSON, *"HOPE IS THE THING WITH
FEATHERS,"* 1861

W e have focused on the downside of ambiguity
and on how painfully stressful it is when
combined with loss. Now let's look at its
positive side. There is hope in it.

Seeing the good side of ambiguity gives back to you
some of the control that the dementia has taken away.
Embracing ambiguity's constructive side gives you a
resiliency and strength to endure your caregiving journey.

Delicious ambiguity is a term used by comedian Gilda
Radner, a *Saturday Night Live* veteran.[1] Suffering from
cancer and unsure if she would live or die, her book, *It's
Always Something,* took a philosophical turn. She wrote,

"Now I've learned, the hard way, that some poems don't rhyme, and some stories don't have a clear beginning, middle and end.... Like my life, this book is about not knowing, having to change, taking the moment and making the best of it, without knowing what's going to happen next. Delicious ambiguity."[2] Gilda's words hold wisdom for us all. She learned that she couldn't control the fear and panic, but she could control how she lived each day.

I write this while visiting New York City—the home of *Saturday Night Live*, which is still thriving at Rockefeller Center. But New York is also home to millions of people who struggle every day, contending with ambiguity. They come from all walks of life—from stockbrokers and investors to artists, playwrights, and poets. Life is uncertain, and that's not always bad. If you write poetry, play bingo, go fishing or sailing, participate in the office pool for the Super Bowl or the Academy Awards—or simply enjoy a good mystery book, you already know that ambiguity can be fun. In this way, Gilda was right. Take the moment and make the best of it, even if the outcome is unclear.

Why Do We Need a More Positive View of Ambiguity?

When I talk about ambiguity with people who are caring for someone with dementia, some say that the adjective *delicious* is too strong for their taste. Their objection is understandable. After all, Gilda didn't make it. She died only months after writing those words. Yet caregivers, too, need a catchy term like delicious ambiguity in order to hold on to the positive side of what is so often a painful and threatening experience. The specific choice of adjective is less important than the idea itself. In the ambiguity, there is a shred of hope.

One Sunday morning, I heard journalist and author Krista Tippett announce that her radio program that morning would be titled "Alzheimer's, Memory and Being." I listened intently as her guest, Alan Dienstag, New York psychologist and founder of the Alzheimer's Memory Project, told stories about working with dementia patients to record their memories. This one was about a woman named Ann:

> She was one of those people who started to kind
> of retreat into almost a mask-like blankness. It was
> harder and harder to access her.... And so it was
> around that time, and I was going on vacation,
> and she loved the beach and I loved the beach and
> this was something that we used to connect about.
> And I said to her, as I was leaving, I said, "Ann,
> I'm going to the beach. I'm going to be away for a
> while." And she smiled and her face kind of lit up.
> I said, "What do you love about the beach?" She
> kind of drifted away, as she did, and she got very
> quiet. And again I waited and I thought, well, you
> know, she can't really answer that question. And
> she turned to me and she said, "There's some

kind of music that lives there." And I thought, "Oh, god. That's the best answer."[3]

Such uniquely profound answers remind us that dementia does not destroy everything. Often something remains that is still wonderful. Out of the fog comes surprising wisdom. And if we can let go of our usual way of thinking, what Ann said makes sense. Of course there is some kind of music living in the beautiful places we remember.

With deeper understanding, we are not so afraid anymore of unanswered questions. There is more acceptance of ambiguity, the twin to dementia's loss. Even though a caregiver's pain and anxiety are real, so is the possibility of some good in the altered relationship.

What is it that ambiguity offers? Overall, it opens up possibilities for human growth and strength. Ambiguity also

- Allows for some hope despite our having no guarantee of a desired outcome
- Allows for change and new opportunities for adventure
- Keeps us on our toes, with no room for complacency
- Makes us grow emotionally and spiritually
- Encourages us to be more spontaneous and improvisational in other parts of our lives
- Allows for creative ways to keep loved ones present during the illness and after they have died
- Gives us time to say good-bye and, if necessary, to work out unresolved issues

✤ Gives us time to learn more about ourselves and to feel how strong we really are
✤ Keeps the door open
✤ Teaches us that nothing is final

Ambiguity can be your friend. When your loved one becomes lucid, even for a moment, that brief time can be exquisite pleasure. When you have to make a hard decision and you don't have enough information to guarantee its outcome, ambiguity can justify moving forward. You have nothing to lose, so you can try something new.

This unorthodox kind of thinking might be criticized as too risky, but loving someone with dementia demands it. Like all mysteries, dementia's story holds back the answers. Suspense can energize and pique curiosity about what comes next. This is the upside, but there are, of course, exceptions.

When Ambiguity Is Not Delicious and Never Will Be

Sometimes things don't go so well, and the person you care for may be unhappy or unruly. No matter how creative you are, there are no smiles, no contentment. There may even be abuse toward you. In these cases, ambiguity *never* is delicious. If this is your situation, recognize that the absurdity here lies in the fact that nothing you do seems to help. Then it's up to you, in your own mind, to create a safe space—perhaps even a delicious place—where you know (and even others know) that you have done your best and can do no more.

If your loved one becomes verbally or physically abusive, however, finding the positive side of ambiguity is not always possible. If you must step down from caregiving, you may have to find solace in simply knowing that you did the best you could by finding other people to do the work. Try to become like Helen (whom we met in Chapter Three), who put the hard news in her pocket to deal with later. In the case of abusive words, however, don't take them out again. Leave them there or symbolically discard them. Helen eventually had to listen to the doctor's words, but you don't have to listen to abusive words. Don't let them in. It will be useful to think of the nastiness as the disease talking, but also minimize the time you spend in the line of fire.

The Silver Lining

Although for a few caregivers the ambiguity will never be delicious, for many there are some good moments to be had. What helps you find that silver lining?

Find Your Resiliency

Resiliency has been a major thread throughout this book. It can be an outcome of your difficult journey with dementia. Caregiving can make you stronger.

Resiliency is most easily understood through metaphor—a suspension bridge swaying in a storm, a tree bending in the wind and then bouncing back. But resiliency is more than just flexibility or bounce-back elasticity. It's your becoming stronger due to your many burdens and pressures. Although it is painful, adversity *can* make you stronger.[4]

In the old days, wagon makers knew that the strongest tree was the one most exposed to the elements. The stress of bending back and forth actually built strength.[5] Like a tree tested by the elements, you too can grow stronger, but this requires seeing the upside of loving someone with dementia, not just the downside.

In academic journals, tests of resiliency consistently contain questions about one's tolerance for ambiguity,[6] but clinically, I prefer to test resiliency with more abstract questions: Have you ever walked in the fog? Did you stay calm? How do you feel when you don't know what will come next? Can you be reasonably comfortable even if you don't know what's around the corner? Can you tolerate absurdity, or does it always make you angry?

Laugh at Absurdity

An ability to laugh at the absurdity of ambiguous loss can take away its bitter potency. Ambiguous loss is no longer something to fear. It's no longer something that holds you helpless. You have the power to laugh at mistakes and mishaps. It releases your tension. In that moment, you stop resisting the dementia and its repercussions, and begin to go with the flow—a necessity given the endless work of caregiving.

Carol Connolly, poet laureate of St. Paul, Minnesota, writes of both pain and pleasure during the fifteen years in which she cared for her life partner. Having been a man of the world, he'd often say he was going off to California, and she learned to say, "Have a good trip!" He "traveled" that way often, and it gave them both a smile. She transformed it into poetry: " 'Sweetheart. It is glorious to see you,' he said. 'I plan to leave tomorrow. I will need a coat and a hat.' "[7]

Author Patricia Hampl writes in her memoir, *The Florist's Daughter*, of her mother, who took an imaginary lover as she progressed into dementia. Her mother told her she had a secret and had been "on pins and needles," worried that her daughter would not approve. " 'I married Don today,' she says ... 'Who's Don?' I ask. 'He's the owner of this *ship*' [the nursing home].... 'Do you mind?' ... 'No, it's okay,' I say. Then ... I hear myself saying, 'Is he rich—Don?' "[8]

Like Carol, Patricia finds some humor in absurdity and goes with the flow. She, too, joins the fantasy in a playful way because her loved one likes it, and doing so is less stressful than insisting on reality. Patricia continues, "I tell her we'll go to the coffee shop downstairs for dinner. There is no coffee shop, but I've fallen into the same fictional habits she has now: the lobby with a couple of small tables is 'the coffee shop,' the sidewalk entryway is 'the terrace.' I'm not aware of these fictions between us until I hear myself say them in front of one of the nurses who looks at me strangely."[9] Truth is relative with dementia, but sometimes, just to keep us alert, the truth emerges in unexpected places.

While I was sitting with a group of dementia patients, the group leader asked them, "Why are you here?" She meant, why was the group in this room instead of the room they met in last week? But before she could explain, a participant responded, "Why are we here? Because we're not all here." Everyone laughed! The forthright honesty brought levity to all. Humor, when you can muster it, will ease your stress and pain. Funny movies, funny stories, improvisation, jokes—anything that brings a laugh or smile—is good for you.

Find the Middle Ground Between Reality and Doubt

The fascination with ambiguity and truth is often transformed into art that entertains and makes us think about reality in another way. While suffering from terminal cancer, playwright Wendy Wasserstein composed her final play, *Third*. In it, she cautions us against the arrogance of thinking that we have the absolute truth. Her parting message to us was that we should keep our eyes and ears open to other possibilities because reality is complex.

(Caregivers know this.) She proposed a "third" way to think, beyond the extremes at either end of the continuum. This third way can be likened to both-and thinking.

Wasserstein was writing primarily about left and right extremes in politics, but her third way—embracing the middle ground of compromise and ambiguity—can also help us live better with problems that have no solutions, such as terminal illness.[10] *We* must be curious about the value of ambiguity, too, or we wouldn't make hits out of so many plays and films that center around the subject. Take, for example, the film *Doubt*, which was adapted from a play of the same name. *Doubt* opened on Broadway in a theater full of New York's leaders and celebrities—the head of a network sat behind me, an Academy Award winner in front of me. All were masters of their trade; we would expect them to prefer certainty to doubt, mastery to uncertainty. After the play and rousing applause, the play's author, John Patrick Shanley, spoke to the audience. "We've got to learn to live with a full measure of uncertainty. There is no last word. That's the silence under the chatter of our time."[11]

To live with the uncertainty and ambiguity, you have to think about your own nature and who you are. If you're the type who insists on certainty arrived at through clear, coherent reasoning, you'll have a harder time. Simply reading about ambiguity might not suffice to increase your comfort with it, so I prescribe other ways—seeing films, going to plays or art exhibits, enjoying improvisational comedy. Why? Because creative artists and writers have for centuries acknowledged the complexities of doubt and ambiguity. It is a favorite theme. Today artists still illuminate ambiguity in their work. They don't let it devastate them.

Develop a Broad Spiritual Worldview

For people living with dementia, there is ambiguity in diagnosis, prognosis, and relationships. To make sense of things, you need a more spiritual worldview. It may or may not be connected to religion. What's important is for your view of how the world works to include the acceptance of *not* knowing the answers to all questions or problems.

Although spirituality means different things to different people, I define it more generally as having tolerance for ambiguity—and becoming comfortable with it.[12] Despite "not knowing," you have the confidence or faith that things will work out.

What I have learned from the thousands of families I have worked with is that regardless of its source, a higher tolerance for ambiguity reduces stress and anxiety. For some, their faith in the unknown involves God; for others, it's nature; but for all, it's an understanding—a meaning—that they don't have to require certainty all the time. Accepting that idea helps calm people down.

To develop a broader spiritual worldview means being mindful of what can't be solved. You accept not having answers all the time and are at ease with the ambiguity. This view is very helpful when someone you love has dementia. Interestingly, it's now being used in the world of business management as a means of handling complex situations.[13] Anyone who takes care of a loved one who has dementia deals daily with complex situations and ambiguity—and would have some good advice to offer here.

Embrace Negative Capability

To see the good in ambiguity—and to underpin the previous discussion—let's consider the term *negative capability*.[14] This concept, based on a term coined by John Keats, the nineteenth-century poet, can help you live with your ambiguous loss.

John Keats loved mystery, and he wrote to his brothers with perhaps the most positive spin on ambiguity. He valued the capability to embrace ambiguity and called it a "negative capability." He believed people were "capable of being in uncertainties, mysteries, doubts, without any irritable reaching after fact and reason."[15] If someone you love has dementia, you will need to have some negative capability.

Keats believed that we all have the ability to accept uncertainties—that not every question has to have an answer and that not every problem has to be resolved—and that uncertainties are places to more fully understand your existence and who you are. I believe this, too. Even today—perhaps especially today—we have the capability to see some good in the ambiguity we first saw as terrible.

Negative capability gives us the ability to embrace the mysteries that life has given us—dementia being only one of them. It allows us to let things go, without feeling guilty about not being able to make them better.

Face the Terror of Dementia

To see the upside of ambiguity, we first have to look at its darkest side: the pervasive denial of death in our culture, in addition to what is called death anxiety.[16] But perhaps, before we can be terrified of death, we experience "dementia anxiety." We are terrified by the idea of memories being wiped away. The possibility of forgetting horrifies us. We may unconsciously stay away from dementia patients and their caregivers because we are too anxious to face what we fear—oblivion.

Though scientists are making progress on the possibilities of cure or prevention, the fear of dementia is valid for the moment. Yet it should not immobilize us. To understand the whole picture of caregiving, we look at the good and the bad.

Why is it we are so terrorized by dementia? Perhaps we need to face what most of us prefer to avoid: our own anxiety about death and fading away. This very personal exploration should not, however, become a preoccupation. As Irvin Yalom, Professor Emeritus of Psychiatry at Stanford University, writes in his book *Staring at the Sun: Overcoming the Terror of Death*: "It's like trying to stare the sun in the face: you can stand only so much of it."[17]

Although we can bear only so much when thinking about a loved one or ourselves fading away, we cannot avoid the topic. We must take a moment now and then to become aware of our anxiety about death and disappearance. Once we are more mindful of this, we will be more able to manage the fear or to ask a professional to help us do so.

What I have learned through my therapy practice—and as a family member—is that there is ultimately more comfort in facing our anxieties than in denying them. Don't hide your fears. Talk with someone about them. Indeed, the "antidote to much anguish is sheer connectedness."[18] To calm your anxiety, spend time with someone who can be there for you—another caregiver or a sibling, friend, neighbor, therapist, counselor, or clergy member. People are terrified by what they cannot understand, but meaning and hope are most easily found in the company of others.

Try to live more existentially.[19] This means accepting the idea that suffering is part of human existence and that such experience is unique to each individual. Existence does not result from unconscious desire but from the *meaning* you give to your experience—despite its complexity. Scientists may not be able to measure this kind of reality, but it is *real* to you. For you, living more existentially means living more fully in the moment rather than in the past or future. The present may be all there is for you because the past and its memories have been wiped out by your loved one's dementia, and the future is unclear. Your existence with dementia is not a rational experience.

Despite the terror and absurdity, give your life meaning beyond the role of caregiving. Recognize hopelessness and despair and risk some changes. Live each day as it comes. Become more aware of your fears and joys, and know who you are. Become aware of the ambiguity and how you might manage the stress of it. Don't shy away from it. Look straight at dementia—and death; once you recognize the source of your terror, you are more able to cope with it.

■ ■

Your losses from dementia may be terrifying and may never make complete sense to you, but you can manage if you remember that the culprit is the ambiguity and that your feelings of confusion and doubt are not signs of weakness or failure on your part. Knowing this gives you permission to let go of trying to find the perfect solution. It gives you permission to stop trying to fix things and instead just to do the best you can. A friend said, "Having permission to *not* find a solution has helped me to enjoy the time I do spend with my mom—just as she is and who she is now. It's liberating." Accepting the paradox helps us find hope.

When you love someone with dementia, your existence is not an issue of rational thinking but of being able to see some wonder and delight at times in your relationship. When you see some good moments—perhaps even delicious moments—you are no longer captive to the terror.

⟪ *Ideas for Reflection and Discussion* ⟫

Ambiguity is stressful, but it can also be a source of positivity. Think about the following ideas and, ideally, discuss with them others:

* ✷ Be resilient; decide to see some good, not just the bad, in the dementia and its ambiguity.

* ✷ When you embrace the good, you have extra flexibility—a broader array of coping strategies—to withstand the pressures of caregiving.

* ✷ To see the upside of ambiguous loss requires imagination, curiosity, and creativity.

* ✷ You can actually grow stronger from withstanding the pressure of caregiving.

* ✷ There is both terror and humor in the ambiguity associated with dementia, and it is useful to find humor in a sad situation.

❋ No one has ever faced your particular situation before, so feel free to improvise. Just do what comes to you as the right thing to do.

❋ Be spontaneous; be flexible enough to shift your view on a dime. What you planned today may not work; go with the flow.

❋ Accept the mystery; become curious about your situation. No one knows for sure what it is, so be observant, curious, analytical—all the things that you read about in detective stories.

❋ Find spirituality. It doesn't have to be only the religious kind. Find more capability for embracing ambiguous situations; develop some trust in the unknown.

❋ We can learn about the deliciousness and absurdity of ambiguity through many different forms of art—literature, comedy, film, theater, music.

❋ A loving relationship is both painful and pleasant. The more deeply you care, the harder it is to say good-bye.

❋ We might not be able to overcome our terror of dementia, but once we understand the real source of our terror, we can more easily cope.

9

The Good-Enough Relationship

Is it a claim that the less good is not exactly the same as the good, yet it has its rights, and must be protected as though it contained a new value? Perhaps it does.

—FLORIDA SCOTT-MAXWELL, *THE MEASURE OF MY DAYS*, *1979, p. 9*

Rarely is there absolute presence or absence in human relationships. Being 100 percent present—emotionally and physically—for someone is rarely possible in mobile societies where family members work outside the home or move away. But if your loved one has dementia, the incongruence between your loved one's absence and presence can be debilitating, if you let it be.

Until there's a cure or a preventive measure for dementia, the only window for change lies within your own thinking. Your perception of a good relationship

155

must shift to a new value: the less good. You can soften your standards of perfection so that you gradually see that a "good-enough" relationship also has a place.

Accepting the idea of a less than perfect relationship is not equivalent to giving up. This type of acceptance is an *active* decision to recognize the reality of a relationship compromised by dementia. You eventually come to an awareness of things as they really are, imperfect and less than ideal,[1] but the emphasis shifts to self-control, and with that, you retain the dignity of free will. It's not about giving up. It's about staying strong and in charge. Valuing a less than perfect relationship is *your* choice.

To make this shift, stop fighting the ambiguity and acknowledge what you still have. If you can still touch the person you love and talk with him, even if the conversation is one-sided; if you can smile with her, even if it's not returned; if you can just be there thoughtfully, it can be good enough. There's a new kind of hope for you in this. You are making this choice, and you're no longer spending precious energy trying to fix something that very likely won't get better. In the case of dementia or any condition that compromises presence, you discover new hope only when you embrace the imperfections of love and caring. Your relationship may not perfect, but you can choose to accept what there still is as "good enough." This part is within your control.

As a therapist, I have been awed many times as I witness this *relational* shift. You can make it, too, but it's not automatic. Once you intentionally change how you see

156

your relationship and, assuming there is no abuse, accept it as it is, you'll feel a peacefulness and strength you never knew you had before.

In learning to accept unanswered questions and to temper your desire for closure, you will find that stress and anxiety diminish, allowing you to cultivate the resiliency to positively endure a relationship with someone who now depends on you for care. If you allow dementia to act as a teacher, of sorts, it shows you that *you* have to change not only your perceptions but also the core of your being. There are lessons in adversity, and you can become stronger if you are willing to change.

Before you can decide to shift into the good-enough relationship, you must be willing to relinquish some of your desire for independence. In our culture, this is not a simple thing to suggest, but many have done it in an effort to preserve themselves as well as the loved one they care for. As we enter midlife, leaning on our partners, children, and friends for help is increasingly necessary—and when we do so, the ideals of self-sufficiency and independence begin to break down.

The Myth of Independence

Despite an aging population, the bar for individual independence is set exceptionally high in our society. Self-sufficiency is assumed and valued to a sometimes dangerous degree. People want to stay "independent" for

157

as long as possible, even if their independence comes with a cost. Even policymakers expect families to take care of their own as long as possible. They do this with little regard to the caregivers, failing to acknowledge that sometimes, keeping a patient out of institutional care comes at the cost of the caregiver's health and independence.

Most of us will eventually become either a caregiver or a care receiver, and when we take on either of these roles, independence becomes a myth. As we cherish independence, we must at the same time cherish *interdependence*. An interdependent relationship is not necessarily an unhealthy one; in fact, it can be just the opposite. This is how families and couples in an aging society will survive.

I recall a conversation I had with Carl Whitaker, the pioneer family therapist and nonconformist I mentioned in Chapter Four. We talked about what was normal in marriage and family life. For a time during my doctoral training at the University of Wisconsin-Madison, I was Whitaker's cotherapist. Whenever I entered his office, I wondered about the strange coffee table that was placed in front of the couch. It was shaped in the design of the yin and yang: two separate halves symbolizing male and female, with each half being able to stand alone (in this case, because each half had three legs) or merge together into one complete circle. It looked homemade. Bad carpentry, I thought. However, what baffled me most was that the two halves of the yin and yang had been heavily bolted together with no pretense of hiding the hardware. I thought this was a corruption of the ancient symbol's meaning.

One day, while waiting for a couple to arrive for therapy, I asked Dr. Whitaker about his table. He said he had in fact made it himself.

I asked, "Why did you bolt the two halves together?"

With his customary brevity, he replied, "When couples get older, it's okay to be fused together."

Back then, I had just turned forty and was imbued with hard-won marital independence. I was in graduate school for a doctorate, studying about the importance of maintaining one's separateness and individuality and the dangers of marital enmeshment. I couldn't understand what Whitaker meant when he said interlocking and fusing together was okay.[2] I pushed the issue now and then, but it became apparent to me that he and his wife, Muriel, were indeed one. All of us who studied with him in his later years knew how close they were to one another. In the end, he didn't even do therapy without her.

Now in my seventies—the same age Carl was when he bolted those yin and yang halves together to create his coffee table—I know what he meant. My husband and I depend on each other's help quite often. I lean on him when my back goes out; he leans on me when his rheumatoid arthritis flares. Yet we continue to see ourselves as fiercely independent individuals. We smile at the paradox: it's our *interdependence* that allows us to be *independent*.

■ ■

Independence becomes less attainable as you grow older. Out of necessity, interdependency becomes the norm. One partner depends on the other, or a parent depends on an adult child; first, for driving, paying bills, and managing medications, and later for more: dressing, feeding, drinking, toileting, and transferring from bed to chair and back again, day after day, year after year. Survival depends on a person's willingness to always be there to meet the needs of the other. But here's the rule for caregivers: that person cannot always be the *same* person. It cannot always be you, or you will burn out. Arrange for others to fill in so that you can take a breather and get some rest and recreation.

Why Do People Give Care?

In a society that values self-sufficiency, having your destiny fused to someone else, someone who is not at all self-sufficient, can be traumatizing. You feel helpless. Like the halves of Whitaker's coffee table, you are locked together with the person you care for, unable to have the freedom you had before. It's not fusion in the usual psychological sense; rather, it's a relational adaptation that must occur because your loved one can't survive alone. Unless there is someone to help or take over, you are indeed stuck.

Without you, the relationship has no stability. It's messy and sometimes not even good enough. So why do people continue to care?

People give care for a variety of reasons. One caregiver, the poet Carol Connolly, told me there was still much good in her relationship:

> A lot of my loved one's 15 years with dementia were very positive for me, and my presence seemed always to be a positive thing for him. I miss him very much in both of his modes, pre and post. There was much good in both.

Another caregiver told me she wanted to do the right thing:

> I feel that I live part of my life in a place that's cloudy. But I am not waiting for my mate to die anymore. I got lost in the ambiguity, I know I did. But I got myself back. I wanted to do the right thing, but it took a while to figure out what that was.

Still another didn't know why she continued to give care:

> Even I wonder why I can sit daily by his side as I play tapes, relate bits and pieces of news, hold his hand, tell him I love him. Yet I am content when I am with him, though I grieve for the loss of his smile, the sound of my name on his lips.

What we know is that a caregiver's journey is psychologically painful, physically exhausting, and long. Many

161

give care primarily for love and duty; others tell me that they do the caregiving themselves because other options are too costly or because society expects it of them. For a variety of reasons, the pressures on family members to take care of dementia patients *at home* is huge—and millions have accepted that role.

Nel Noddings, a Stanford professor who wrote about the ethics of caring, says that the act of caregiving doesn't fit psychology's theories of motivation, because it goes beyond the motivations of self-preservation and profit.[3] People give care even if doing so is not in their best interests.

What is it then that makes caregivers continue even when their own finances and health are in jeopardy? These are typical responses I hear: "I promised 'in sickness and health, till death do us part,' so I'm going to honor that promise" or "I believe in 'honoring thy father and mother,' so I take care of them." Still others say they give care because they think it's simply the right thing to do.

Whatever it is that motivates caregivers may still be a mystery. Perhaps their motivations are understood best through love, but scientists have trouble with that concept, as it's not easily measured. But I see love often—in my office, in workshops, in nursing homes, even in the mall when an old man pauses to help his demented wife who can't find her way on her own anymore. What is born out of love and empathy, even if they are mixed with obligation, is called caring, and it's one of the most valuable resources we have in an aging society.

The Downside: When "Good Enough" Doesn't Work

When there has been abuse from the person who now requires your care, the good-enough relationship, understandably, may not be for you. If there was incest, abuse, or abandonment, you may want to give up on the relationship altogether.

Taking care of someone who years before was abusive or neglectful of you is beyond what is expected of you. Caring for a family member who was or is physically or psychologically abusive is dangerous. Feeling as if you want to retaliate is also dangerous. These are justifiable reasons for *not* being a caregiver.

Talk with someone about your options. Other people can do the hands-on work. If the patient is financially able, set up a plan for professional care. If not, talk with the county social worker to find out about alternatives.

Each case is different, but with most, I encourage some kind of continued management—often through a social worker—to make sure that the caregiving team or the nursing home professionals are treating your family member well. This may be the best you can do given your history together. Such minimal attention, however, eases ambivalence, anger, and guilt and, overall, fosters your

163

emotional growth. As Nel Noddings wrote, "I do not 'care' for this person. I may hate him, but I need not. If I do something in his behalf ... it is because I care about my own ethical self."[4]

Sometimes even good relationships can't make the shift to patient-caregiver. A colleague told me about such a couple. "It was a marriage of two very strong, autonomous people. They couldn't make the shift to caring—she was too independent to accept care; he too impatient to persuade." "Good enough" was not for them.

If you lack patience, you are not cut out for caregiving; if your loved one is too belligerent and abusive for you to manage, you must find alternatives. Guilt often prevents people from doing the right thing, but here lies the paradox: what you *think* is right may be wrong. Sometimes the right thing for your loved one—and you—is to seek institutional or professional care. Rather than doing the hands-on caregiving, you could visit or, at the least, oversee the care (as I described previously). Your goal is to be humane, but also to prevent yourself from being hurt further.

■ ■

It's important to hear again that challenging line of theologian Karen Armstrong's that I quoted in Chapter Five: "Looking after somebody else means that you have to give yourself away" is referring to ego, not the role of caregiving.[5] Don't give yourself away just because you're a caregiver. Know that there's need for moderation.

What you need to avoid is being isolated in a relationship that may never be reciprocal again. Some measure of yourself has to be preserved and nurtured. Being locked together is *not* what I recommend. Rather, think of the two halves of your relationship as being together, one supporting the other, but at times with other people stepping in to relieve you.

If your adult children refuse to support you as a caregiver or, worse yet, if they only criticize from afar, insist on a family meeting with a family therapist present.[6] Family conflicts with adult children and especially stepchildren can be serious; they can isolate you even more.[7] It's because of this and because caregiving requires overfunctioning in an imbalanced relationship that a psychological family becomes important.

It is easier to accept a good-enough relationship if there is another one in which both "give" and "take" are more balanced. Find people to connect with. Find someone to compensate for the support you are losing or have lost. You, too, need someone to lean on. Everyone does. With a psychological family, you intentionally bring people into your life to regain equilibrium.

Don't aim for perfection. Just do the best you can. If you feel as though it's never enough, know that this feeling is typical for most caregivers. Make your peace with imperfection. Your relationship may be less than perfect, but you still have the power to accept what there is as good enough. That part is within your control.

Ideas for Reflection and Discussion

✿ Because absence and presence are not absolutes in human relationships, most of us are in less than perfect relationships, so we already have some knowledge about how to live with ambiguity.

✿ Accepting the idea of a good-enough relationship is your choice.

✿ Independence in older relationships remains the societal ideal, but is often a myth.

✿ Out of necessity, interdependence becomes the norm in older couples and families.

✿ If there has been abuse or neglect, think twice about becoming a caregiver. There are other options.

✿ The reasons people take on the role of caregiver vary, but in the end, it may be due to love, something difficult for scientists to study, but real nevertheless.

Conclusion

Until there is a cure or prevention, few of us will escape the pain of losing someone we love to dementia. Many of us will experience ambiguous loss when a loved one's mind, memory, awareness, judgment, and even personality are going or gone. When dementia appears, from Alzheimer's or other diseases or conditions, the likelihood of interdependency increases—one person needs care, and the other provides it.

The goal is *not* to regain your independence but rather to stay resilient and healthy in a relationship that is now less than perfect, with a loved one physically present but psychologically absent. Throughout this book, I have encouraged you to stay connected with others as a way to manage the stress. Human connection is necessary for health. A member of the Saturday morning caregiving group at the University of Minnesota shares her thoughts, as well as her husband's words, to sum up: "I have been caring for my husband for over seventeen years as we went through the Alzheimer's journey. He has been in care now for three years—it took me a year after I placed him to come to terms with my feelings. Now he is dying, and I hold on to the words he used to say: 'I want you to move on—find somebody—that is what I would do.'"

With the ideas presented throughout this book, you can learn to manage the stress in the shadow land of dementia. Let go of your need for certainty and absolute answers. Acknowledge your sadness as it ebbs and flows, and talk about it with others. Grieve when you feel the need, and know that there is no need for closure. The more you can embrace the ambiguity of dementia's loss, the less terrifying it is.

Above all, remember to care for yourself. Be mindful of when you need a break. A wise caregiver underscores this point: "I realized I couldn't cure Mother, but I could work on healing myself."[1] Caregiving does not have to destroy your health; it doesn't have to lead to depression and isolation. It can instead lead to emotional growth and a strength you never knew you had before.

When I began this book, my goal was to help you find meaning and hope despite your difficult journey with the ambiguous loss of dementia. If you are accustomed to solving problems, this experience can be especially stressful. The best way to make change and ease your stress lies in your own perceptions and the meaning you give to the situation. Your journey is psychological.

Dementia does not have to be terrifying, but everyone needs to acknowledge the stress of despair and mixed emotions it causes in millions of families today. To manage the tensions, begin learning to think in a new way. It is possible to hold two opposing ideas at the same time—absence and presence, sorrow and joy, anger and hope. All are realities when dementia is involved. Instead of being frustrated or afraid, or fighting against the confusion, embrace the ambiguity and continue to care even when your loved one no longer knows who you are. Paradoxically, this loss can help you know who *you* are. Continuing to participate in a less than perfect relationship requires courage and empathy; it deepens your humanity. And *this* is your source of new hope.

Continuing the Journey

We are now at the end of our journey together, but yours may continue if your struggle with dementia's ambiguous loss is ongoing. Here's a summary of the chapters for you to keep at hand as you move forward.

* Chapter One: For you and your loved one, dementia represents ambiguous or unclear loss. It is one of the most difficult kinds of loss because there can be no closure.

* Chapter Two: Through no fault of your own, dementia leads to complicated grief. Even though the complications do not result from your personal weakness, you may need professional help to distinguish between sadness and depression. It's normal to grieve while your loved one is still alive.

* Chapter Three: Caring for someone who has dementia is stressful. Adopting both-and thinking and learning how to manage the stress are necessary if you are to maintain your resiliency. Resiliency means more than simply bouncing back. It means you can grow stronger from the adversity.

* Chapter Four: The myth is that healthy people will find closure, but the reality is that most people learn to live with grief. We don't forget the people we have loved.

- Chapter Five: We live in one of the most individualistic cultures in the world, yet relationships remain the source of our happiness.[2] Sometimes we need a psychological family. Human connection keeps us healthy.
- Chapter Six: Family rituals, celebrations, and gatherings help us make sense of our usual losses and grief, but when you are living with dementia, the loss and grief are ongoing. Create new rituals for this kind of loss.
- Chapter Seven: Discuss with others the seven guidelines for a journey with dementia. In no particular order, consider ideas about meaning, mastery, identity, ambivalence, attachment, hope—and caring for oneself.
- Chapter Eight: Being able to see the good side of the ambiguity in your relationship gives you the resiliency to endure the emotional and physical work of caring for someone with dementia. Live each day as it comes, make the best of it, and laugh when you can. In some cases, there is no good side, so consider other options.
- Chapter Nine: When you love someone with dementia, the goal is not perfection. The new standard for your relationship is simply for it to be good enough. Life with dementia can be less than ideal and still be pretty good. That perceptual shift is under your control.

A Note to Caregivers About Working with Health Care Professionals

I want to add a note about what I hear in workshops, groups, and in my clinical work about the relationship between medical professionals and caregivers. This relationship can be strained, but remember that both parties are working hard on behalf of the same ill person.

I have already written a book for professionals encouraging them to team with families,[1] so here, I talk with you.

As a family caregiver, you need to be acknowledged and treated as part of the health management team for dementia patients. Toward this end, you and the medical professionals with whom you work need to be more aware of each other. This mutual awareness may not bring perfect solutions, but it will lessen frustration—and in the end, the person with dementia benefits.

Medical Professionals

The caregiving relationship challenges everything most of us in the health professions were taught about normal human relationships (see Chapter Nine to revisit Carl Whitaker's coffee table). As a result, a caregiver may be viewed in a negative light—too connected, too emotional, too anxious or depressed. As one nurse said to me when I responded to my anxious mother's phone call by visiting her after her bedtime, "You're feeding off of each other!" Her remark felt like a slap in the face. I had just driven six hours from St. Paul, Minnesota, to southern Wisconsin, and didn't get there in time for regular nursing home visiting hours. Mom was worried and called me—so when I did arrive, I went to reassure her and say goodnight.

Most professionals, including me, have been trained to see enmeshment as pathological, and I believe that the nurse saw our interaction that night—a daughter responding to her mother's call—as just that. No doubt she was trained to see it that way, but today, psychologists such as Robert-Jay Green and Paul Werner can document how such professional views unfairly diagnose caregivers.[2]

As a caregiver, you are, by definition, overly responsive; your job demands that. This responsiveness is embodied in terms that many professionals have been trained to see negatively: *co-dependent, enmeshed,* and *undifferentiated without a sense of self,* among others. Such terms are, however, very harmful to people who care for

174

others—whether it be for the newborn, disabled, dying, or demented. Caregivers should not be pathologized for the work society expects them to do.

I wrote about Deborah, a caregiver to her physician husband, in Chapter Six. Even as a psychologist working in a medical clinic, she had a bad experience. In her case, the issue was safety. She said,

> Professionals focus only on the patient: They give the diagnosis without consideration for the safety of the caregiver. Some physicians will talk to the caregiver about their own welfare, but most consider them superfluous. The caregiver is not their patient so is none of their concern. This attitude, born in the interest of professionalism and patient privacy, has to change when patients are cognitively impaired and still living at home. Physicians and nurses should see the family as part of the team. As yet, most do not.

Another caregiver also had a bad experience and then finally found support:

> Professionals didn't help me to help my husband face reality. The doctors diminished his state of mind and his violence. One doctor told us that we just needed more marriage counseling! I pleaded. Finally, a doctor told him—in my presence, "You have sub-cortical MS, and it's going to get worse." I thanked her because she was the only doctor who would tell us what we were facing.

To be sure, strict rules regarding patient privacy may have prevented most of her husband's doctors from sharing information with her, but there may have been other reasons for withholding, based on training. Few physicians who treat dementia patients are trained to calm worried or distraught caregivers or to talk with (often contentious) families. Fewer yet are given the time to do so.

Caregivers, therefore, need their *own* doctor. Find a primary doctor, family physician, or medical provider who is trained to talk with you and has some time allotted to do so. It is with such medical professionals, not with your loved one's specialist, that you will find *your* advocate. A family practice doctor told me this:

> My patients have often brought caregiving issues up. It may be during a physical or a bronchitis visit, but if it comes up, we discuss it. I've told plenty of caregivers who won't or don't feel they can ask for help from other family or friends to tell them I said they needed help and that they should tell their family members that I was to blame, that it was their doctor who said they weren't able to do it all by themselves anymore. This way a caregiver didn't have to feel guilty or take the heat for asking for help. Or I've told adult child caregivers not to wait for their siblings to offer help, but rather, just call a meeting to organize and delegate tasks. I know the doctors I work with do this sort of thing all the time.

If there's no signature that says we can talk to a daughter or son, we try to facilitate getting that signature or at least talking to whomever is listed so they can relay information. Generally speaking, the doctors that I have worked with over the past twenty years are more apt to try and be helpful than be a roadblock to caregivers.

Mental Health Professionals

Psychotherapists too may not have been trained to take caregivers into account. Although the idea of balance in marriage and family relationships was denounced in the late 1980s,[3] much of therapy training still promotes the view that if one person is symptomatic, the other must be gaining some benefit from keeping him or her that way. As a result, roles where overfunctioning occurs (such as yours) may still be viewed in a negative light.[4]

With some therapists even today, you might arouse suspicion about your mental health if you give up your independence for the sake of the patient, if you have to intrude on personal boundaries in order to do essential personal care when your loved one cannot, if you lose yourself in the "36-hour day,"[5] or if you reverse generational boundaries when you have to care for your parent. But here's the reality: when you are caregiving for a person with dementia, what was formerly considered dysfunctional is now normal.

Depression

Whereas sadness is inevitable for most caregivers, depression is not. Rather than always assuming that a caregiver has depression, some professionals are considering the more benign diagnoses of "adjustment disorder" or "relational problem."[6] Surely, dementia impairs relationships, but this is not the same as caregiver illness. Talk with your doctor or therapist about this.

Not all caregivers feel as negatively about the diagnosis of depression as Mary, the caregiver I mentioned in Chapter Seven, did, but many have told me they resent being labeled as "sick." What I see then is guilt and shame—and feelings of inadequacy, the exact opposite of what a caregiver should feel.

What you need to know is that your environment (caring for someone who has dementia) can create symptoms in even the strongest people. Tell your own doctor or therapist about the reality of your life. If he or she won't listen, ask for someone who will. A family practice doctor, a primary doctor, or a nurse practitioner is more likely to listen than your loved one's specialist. Be honest about how you feel. If you are sad and feel as if you are grieving, tell your *own* doctor. If you feel overwhelmed, hopeless, and depressed, tell your *own* doctor. If you are sleep deprived, tell him or her about your situation. You may not have insomnia; rather, it may be that you are disturbed nightly by your loved one's demands or wandering, or you may be afraid to sleep for fear of something bad happening. Your own medical professionals won't know what's going on around you unless you tell them.

■ ■

Overall, what your professionals need to know is that you are now caught in a relationship that is ambiguous and unbalanced. This *requires* overfunctioning. As in Whitaker's coffee table, one side keeps the other half stable. Antidepressants are not always the answer. Human connection and understanding are also therapeutic—with professionals as well as in private life.

As a caregiver, you need the people in your life, including the professionals, to be more understanding of the sheer complexity of your daily existence. Your journey of trying to do the right thing in an untenable situation is long and hard, and you deserve more acknowledgment. Tell your story. No one else can.

Resources

This section provides a listing of various resources that will help you think about and discuss with others the ideas in this book. I share with you some readings, films, and Web sites that may be helpful. All are meant to aid you in finding hope while coping with the stress and grief that dementia causes in your relationship.

Suggestions for Caregiver Discussion Groups and Book Clubs

Use the bulleted material at the end of each chapter as a discussion guide. The ideas or questions presented there can be used for several meetings. Go slowly; allow for listening, speaking, talking with each other, and just being together.

If you're a homebound caregiver and it's difficult for you to meet with others in person, consider a virtual book club. See www.ambiguousloss.com for more information.

Workshops for Caregivers

See www.ambiguousloss.com to contact me or to view my publications list and speaking and workshop schedule.

Selected Readings

Bayley, J. (1999). *Elegy for Iris*. New York: Picador.

Berman, C. (2005). *Caring for Yourself While Caring for Your Aging Parents: How to Help, How to Survive*. New York: Henry Holt.

Boss, P. (1999). *Ambiguous Loss: Learning to Live with Unresolved Grief*. Boston: Harvard University Press.

Boss, P. (2002). *Family Stress Management: A Contextual Approach* (2nd ed.). Thousand Oaks, CA: Sage.

Boss, P. (2006). *Loss, Trauma, and Resilience: Therapeutic Work with Ambiguous Loss*. New York: Norton.

Davis, P. (2004). *The Long Goodbye*. New York: Knopf.

Goldman, C. (2002). *The Gifts of Caregiving*. Minneapolis, MN: Fairview Press.

Greutzner, H. (2001). *Alzheimer's: A Caregiver's Guide and Source Book*. Hoboken, NJ: Wiley.

Hampl, P. (2007). *The Florist's Daughter*. Orlando, FL: Harcourt.

Kane, R. L. (2011). *The Good Caregiver*. New York: Avery.

Kushner, H. S. (2004). *When Bad Things Happen to Good People*. New York: Anchor.

Lewis, R. W. (Ed.). *Caregiver's Support Kit*. National Caregiving Foundation (1-800-930-1357). Free to caregivers.

Mace, N., and Raskins, P. (2006). *The 36-Hour Day*. Baltimore, MD: Johns Hopkins University Press.

Mayo Clinic. (2006) *Mayo Clinic Guide to Alzheimer's Disease*. Rochester, MN: Mayo Clinic.

McLeod, B. W. (1999). *Caregiving: The Spiritual Journey of Love, Loss, and Renewal*. Hoboken, NJ: Wiley.

Qualls, S. H., and Zarit, S. H. (2009). *Aging Families and Caregiving*. Hoboken, NJ: Wiley.

Rodgers, A. B. (2008). *Alzheimer's Disease: Unraveling the Mystery*. Silver Spring, MD: Alzheimer's Disease Education and Referral Center.

Russo, F. (2010). *They're Your Parents, Too! How Siblings Can Survive Their Parents' Aging Without Driving Each Other Crazy*. New York: Bantam.

Sheehy, G. (2010). *Passages in Caregiving: Turning Chaos into Confidence*. New York: HarperCollins.

Shenk, D. (2003). *The Forgetting: Alzheimer's: Portrait of an Epidemic*. New York: Anchor.

Films About Caregiving and Ambiguous Loss Relationships

Age Old Friends, 1989 (friend has dementia; do I leave him?)

Alzheimer's: What Every African-American Needs to Know (Mayo Clinic, Jacksonville, FL); available at http://alzonline.phhp.ufl.edu/en/videos/124.php, or call 904-953-7103

A Song for Martin, 2001 (caregiving); Swedish film with English subtitles

Aurora Borealis, 2006 (grandfather with dementia)

Away from Her, 2007 (Alzheimer's disease and husband's
  distress)

Complaints of a Dutiful Daughter, 1995 (daughter caregiving
  for mother with Alzheimer's)

Firefly Dreams, 2001 (young caregiver resists and then con-
  nects with woman who has Alzheimer's); Japanese film
  with English subtitles

Iris: A Memoir of Iris Murdoch, 2001 (loving couple and
  dementia)

Is Anybody There? 2009 (friendship of young boy and older
  man with dementia)

The Forgetting: A Portrait of Alzheimer's, 2008 (PBS series
  based on the book *The Forgetting*, by David Shenk)

The Notebook, 2004 (love and dementia, also a book)

The Savages, 2007 (siblings dealing with parental dementia)

Web Sites for Caregivers

Administration on Aging (www.aoa.gov)

Alzheimer's Association (national) (www.alz.org)

Alzheimer's Association Carefinder (www.alz.org/
  carefinder/index.asp)

Alzheimer's Disease and Educational Referral Center
  (www.nia.nih.gov/alzheimers)

American Association of Retired Persons (AARP)
  (www.aarp.org)

American Psychological Association Family Caregiver
  Briefcase (www.apa.org/pi/about/publications/
  caregivers/index.aspx)

Creutzfeldt-Jakob Disease Foundation, Inc.
(www.cjdfoundation.org)

Dementia Advocacy and Support Network
(www.dasninternational.org/index.php)

Eldercare Locator (www.eldercare.gov/Eldercare.NET/
Public/Index.aspx)

Family Caregiving 101 (www.familycaregiving101.org/)

Family Caregiver Alliance (www.caregiver.org)

Family Caregiving Resources Clearinghouse
(http://web.raffa.com/nac/axa/)

HBO—the Alzheimer's Project (www.hbo.com/
alzheimers/index.html)

Huntington's Disease Society of America (www.hdsa.org)

Levy Body Dementia Association (www.lbda.org)

Mayo Clinic (www.MayoClinic.com)

National Academy of Elder Law Attorneys (NAELA)
(www.naela.org)

National Alliance for Caregiving (www.caregiving.org)

National Association of Area Agencies on Aging
(www.n4a.org/)

National Caregivers Library (www.caregiverslibrary.org/)

National Family Caregivers Association (www.nfcacares.org)

National Institute on Aging (NIA) (www.nih.gov/nia)

Notes

Preface

1. P. Boss, ed., "Special Issue: Ambiguous Loss," *Family Relations 56*, no. 2 (April 2007); S. Robins, "Ambiguous Loss in a Non-Western Context: Families of the Disappeared in Postconflict Nepal," *Family Relations 59*, no. 3 (July 2010): 253–268.

Introduction

1. Alzheimer's Association, *2011 Alzheimer's Disease Facts and Figures* (Chicago: Alzheimer's Association National Office, 2011), 12. See L. E. Hebert, P. A. Scherr, J. L. Bienias, D. A. Bennett, and D. A. Evans, "Alzheimer's Disease in the U.S. Population: Prevalence Estimates Using the 2000 Census," *Archives of Neurology 60* (2003): 1119–1122; Alzheimer's Association, *Early-Onset Dementia: A National Challenge, a Future Crisis* (Washington, DC: Alzheimer's Association, June 2006). Available at www.alz.org.

2. Alzheimer's Association, *2011 Alzheimer's Disease Facts and Figures*, 14. See L. E. Hebert, L. A. Beckett, P. A. Scherr, and D. A. Evans, "Annual Incidence of Alzheimer's Disease in the United States Projected to the Years 2000 Through 2050," *Alzheimer's Disease and Associated Disorders 15* (2001): 169–173.

3. Alzheimer's Association, *2011 Alzheimer's Disease Facts and Figures*, 14. See Hebert, Beckett, Scherr, and Evans, "Annual Incidence of Alzheimer's Disease."

4. Alzheimer's Association, *2011 Alzheimer's Disease Facts and Figures*, 12. See S. Seshadri, P. A. Wolf, A. Beiser, R. Au, K. McNulty, R. White, and R. B. D'Agostino, "Lifetime Risk of Dementia and Alzheimer's Disease: The Impact of Mortality on Risk Estimates in the Framingham Study," *Neurology 49* (1997): 1498–1504; L. E. Hebert, P. A. Scherr, J. J. McCann, L. A. Beckett, and D. A. Evans, "Is the Risk of Developing Alzheimer's Disease Greater for Women Than for Men?" *American Journal of Epidemiology 153*, no. 2 (2001): 132–136.

5. Alzheimer's Association, *2011 Alzheimer's Disease Facts and Figures*, 10.

6. Ibid., 27.

7. Ibid., 25. See *2009 National Alliance for Care-giving/AARP Survey on Caregiving in the United States* (Bethesda, MD: National Alliance for Caregiving and Washington, DC: AARP, 2009); data were prepared for the Alzheimer's Association under contract with Matthew Greenwald and Associates, November 11, 2009. See also MetLife Mature Market Institute, *The MetLife Study of Alzheimer's Disease: The Caregiving Experience* (New York: MetLife Mature Market, 2006), www.maturemarketinstitute.com.

8. Alzheimer's Association, *2011 Alzheimer's Disease Facts and Figures*, 25. See in particular Figure 6, "Ages of Alzheimer's and Other Dementia Caregivers, 2010."

9. B. Almberg, M. Grafstrom, and B. Winblad, "Caring for a Demented Elderly Person—Burden and Burnout Among Caregiving Relatives," *Journal of Advanced Nursing 25*, no. 1 (1977): 109–116; S. H. Zarit, P. A. Todd, and J. M. Zarit, "Subjective Burden of Husbands and Wives as Caregivers: A Longitudinal Study," *Gerontologist 26*, no. 3 (1986): doi:10.1093/geront/26.3.260; R. F. Coen, C. A. O'Boyle, D. Coakley, and B. A. Lawlor, "Individual Quality of Life Factors Distinguishing Low-Burden and High-Burden Caregivers of

Dementia Patients," *Dementia and Geriatric Cognitive Disorders 13*, no. 3 (2002): 164–170.

10. N. L. Mace and P. V. Rabins, *The 36-Hour Day* (Baltimore, MD: Johns Hopkins University Press, 2006). (Originally published 1981.)

11. Centers for Disease Control and Prevention, "Caregiving for Alzheimer's Disease or Other Dementia," November 16, 2009, www.cdc.gov/aging/caregiving/alzheimer.htm.

12. Mayo Clinic, "Dementia: Causes," April 17, 2009, www.mayoclinic.com/health/dementia/DS01131/DSECTION=causes.

Chapter 1: The Ambiguous Loss of Dementia

1. *Ambiguous loss* is a term I coined in the 1970s. For references, see www.ambiguousloss.com. For books that summarize the research and application, see P. Boss, *Ambiguous Loss: Learning to Live with Unresolved Grief* (Cambridge, MA: Harvard University Press, 1999) and P. Boss, *Loss, Trauma, and Resilience: Therapeutic Work with Ambiguous Loss* (New York: Norton, 2006). For more recent research on various topics of ambiguous loss, see *Family Relations 56*, no. 2 (April 2007); note especially R. Blieszner, K. A. Roberto, K. L. Wilcox,

E. J. Barham, and B. L. Winston, "Dimensions of Ambiguous Loss in Couples Coping with Mild Cognitive Impairment," 196–209.

2. S. Roos, *Chronic Sorrow: A Living Loss* (New York: Brunner-Routledge, 2002).

3. C. Feigelson, "Personality Death, Object Loss, and the Uncanny," *International Journal of Psychoanalysis* 74, no. 2 (1993): 331–345.

4. R. J. Waldinger and M. S. Schulz, "What's Love Got to Do with It? Social Functioning, Perceived Health, and Daily Happiness in Married Octogenarians," *Psychology and Aging 25*, no. 2 (June 2010): 422–431.

5. R. Schulz and S. Beach, "Caregiving as a Risk Factor for Mortality: The Caregiver Health Effects Study," *Journal of the American Medical Association 282*, no. 3 (December 15, 1999): 2215–2219. See also R. Schulz and L. M. Martire, "Family Caregiving of Persons with Dementia: Prevalence, Health Effects, and Support Strategies," *American Journal of Geriatric Psychiatry 12*, no. 3 (May-June 2004): 240–249.

Chapter 2: The Complications of Both Loss and Grief

1. American Psychiatric Association, *Diagnostic and Statistical Manual of Mental Disorders*, 4th ed., text revision (Washington, DC: American Psychiatric Association, 2000), 741.

2. Ibid., 737.

3. *The New Shorter Oxford English Dictionary*, 4th ed., s.v. "Grief."

4. Ibid., s.v. "Bereavement."

5. E. Lindemann, "Symptomatology and the Management of Acute Grief," *Journal of Psychiatry 101* (1944): 141–148.

6. M. deVries, "Trauma in Cultural Perspective," in *Traumatic Stress: The Effects of Overwhelming Experience on Mind, Body, and Society*, ed. B. A. van der Kolk, A. C. MacFarlane, and L. Weisaeth (New York: Guilford Press, 2007), 404.

7. E. Kübler-Ross, *On Death and Dying* (New York: MacMillan, 1969).

8. In her second book, *On Grief and Grieving* (New York: Scribner, 2005), this one based on less research, Kübler-Ross stated that her five stages of grief developed for the dying would also apply to people who are in mourning.

9. M. O'Rourke, "Good Grief," *New Yorker*, February 1, 2010, 66.

10. See E. Kübler-Ross, *The Wheel of Life* (New York: Touchstone, 1997). In this memoir, Kübler-Ross discusses this messiness and her bitterness and defiance.

11. G. A. Bonanno, *The Other Side of Sadness* (New York: Basic, 2009).

12. D. S. Becvar, *In the Presence of Grief: Helping Family Members Resolve Death, Dying, and Bereavement Issues* (New York: Guilford Press, 2001); Bonanno, *Other Side of Sadness;* P. Boss, *Ambiguous Loss: Learning to Live with Unresolved Grief* (Cambridge, MA: Harvard University Press, 1999); P. Boss, *Loss, Trauma, and Resilience: Therapeutic Work with Ambiguous Loss* (New York: Norton, 2006); P. Boss, "The Trauma and Complicated Grief of Ambiguous Loss," *Pastoral Psychology 59*, no. 2 (2010): 137–145.

13. K. Doka, *Disenfranchised Grief: New Directions, Challenges, and Strategies for Practice* (Champaign, IL: Research Press, 2002).

Chapter 3: Stress, Coping, and Resiliency

1. R. T. Kasuya, P. Polgar-Bailey, and R. Takeuchi, "Caregiver Burden and Burnout: A Guide for Primary Care Physicians," *Postgraduate Medicine 108*, no. 7 (December 2000): 119–123. Referenced in L. Etters, D. Goodall, and B. E. Harrison, "Caregiver Burden Among Dementia Patient Caregivers: A Review of the Literature," *Journal of the American Academy of Nurse Practitioners 20*, no. 8 (August 2008): 423–428.

2. A. A. Atienza, P. C. Henderson, S. Wilcox, and A. C. King, " Gender Differences in Cardiovascular

Response to Dementia Caregiving," *Gerontologist 41*, no. 4 (2001): doi:10.1093/geront/41.4.490; C. Donaldson and A. Burns, "Burden of Alzheimer's Disease: Helping the Patient and Caregiver," *Geriatric Psychiatry and Neurology 12*, no. 1 (April 1999): doi: 10.1177/089198879901200106. Both referenced in N. R. Chumbler, J. W. Grimm, M. Cody, and C. Beck, "Gender, Kinship and Caregiver Burden: The Case of Community-Dwelling Memory Impaired Seniors," *International Journal of Geriatric Psychiatry 18*, no. 8 (August 2003): 722–732.

3. B. J. Kramer and E. H. Thompson Jr., eds., *Men as Caregivers* (Amherst, MA: Prometheus Books, 2005).

4. National Alliance for Caregiving and AARP, *Caregiving in the U.S.* (Bethesda, MD: National Alliance for Caregiving and Washington, DC: AARP, 2004); MetLife Mature Market Institute, *The MetLife Study of Sons at Work Balancing Employment and Eldercare* (New York: Metropolitan Life Insurance Company, 2003).

5. J. L. Yee and R. Schulz, "Gender Differences in Psychiatric Morbidity Among Family Caregivers: A Review and Analysis," *Gerontologist 40* (2000): 147–164; M. Navaie-Waliser, A. Spriggs, and P. H. Feldman, "Informal Caregiving: Differential Experiences by Gender," *Medical Care 40* (2002): 1249–1259.

6. National Alliance for Caregiving and AARP, *Caregiving in the U.S.*; L.M.B. Alecxih, S. Zeruld, and B. Olearczyk, *Characteristics of Caregivers Based on the Survey of Income and Program Participation* (Falls Church, VA: Lewin Group, 2001).

7. Family Caregiver Alliance, *Selected Caregiver Statistics*, revised 2005, www.caregiver.org/caregiver/jsp/content_node.jsp?nodeid=439.

8. N. G. Cuellar, "Comparison of African American and Caucasian American Female Caregivers of Rural, Post-Stroke, Bedbound Older Adults," *Gerontological Nursing 28* (2002): 36–45; W. E. Haley, L. N. Gitlin, S. R. Wisniewski, D. F. Mahoney, D. W. Coon, L. Winter, M. Corcoran, S. Schinfeld, and M. Ory, "Well-Being, Appraisal, and Coping in African-American and Caucasian Dementia Caregivers: Findings from the REACH Study," *Aging and Mental Health 8* (2004): 316–329; M. Pinquart and S. Sorenson, "Ethnic Differences in Stressors, Resources, and Psychological Outcomes of Family Caregiving: A Meta-Analysis," *Gerontologist 45* (2005): 90–106.

9. Pinquart and Sorenson, "Ethnic Differences."

10. Regarding caregiver burden, Etters and colleagues add that "Self-efficacy behaviors may also influence coping strategies"; Etters et al., "Caregiver Burden," 424.

11. Etters et al., "Caregiver Burden."

12. C. W. Sherman and P. Boss, "Spousal Dementia Caregiving in the Context of Late-Life Remarriage," *Dementia: The International Journal of Social Research and Practice 6* (May 2007): 245–270.

13. G. T. Deimling, V. L. Smerglia, and M. L. Schaefer, "The Impact of Family Environment and Decision-Making Satisfaction on Caregiver Depression: A Path Analytic Model," *Aging and Health 13* (2001): doi:10.1177/089826430101300103. Referenced in Etters et al., "Caregiver Burden."

14. H. Lavretsky, "Stress and Depression in Informal Family Caregivers of Patients with Alzheimer's Disease," *Aging Health 1*, no. 1 (2005): 117–133.

15. P. Dilworth-Anderson, P. Y. Goodwin, and S. W. Williams, "Can Culture Help Explain the Physical Health Effects of Caregiving over Time Among African American Caregivers?" *Journal of Gerontology: Social Sciences 59B*, no. 3 (2004): S138–S145; P. Dilworth-Anderson, G. Boswell, and M. D. Cohen, "Spiritual and Religious Coping Values and Beliefs Among African American Caregivers: A Qualitative Study," *Applied Gerontology 26*, no. 4 (2007): 355–369.

16. Etters et al., "Caregiver Burden."

17. Ibid.; F. M. Torti, L. P. Gwyther, S. D. Reed, J. Y. Friedman, and K. A. Schulman, "A Multinational

Review of Recent Trends and Reports in Dementia Caregiver Burden," *Alzheimer's Disease and Associated Disorders 18*, no. 2 (2004): 99–109.

18. Etters et al., "Caregiver Burden"; Torti et al., "A Multinational Review."

19. P. Belluck, "In a Land of Aging, Children Counter Alzheimer's," *New York Times*, November 26, 2010, A1, A12.

20. Faith communities should play an even greater role in sponsoring such support groups. It is important that they are not grief-after-death groups but groups for people like Ruth who must live with ambiguous loss.

Chapter 4: The Myth of Closure

1. C. L. Campbell and A. S. Demi, "Adult Children of Fathers Missing in Action (MIA)," *Family Relations 49* (2000): 267–276.

2. A. de Saint-Exupéry, *The Little Prince* (New York: Harcourt Brace Jovanovich, 1971). (Originally published 1943.) Ironically, a year after this book's publication, the author also went missing as his plane disappeared over the Mediterranean Sea. Life mimicked art. Believe me, *The Little Prince* is not just a children's story. If you love someone who has dementia, you'll find comfort in it.

3. Saint-Exupéry, *Little Prince*, 82, 84.

4. Ibid., 87.

5. Saint-Exupéry, *Little Prince*, 8. This phrase appears on several pages.

6. Ibid., 67.

7. F. Perls, *Gestalt Therapy Verbatim* (Lafayette, CA: Real People Press, 1969). Whereas Perls worked with individuals, Walter Kempler worked with families. Like Whitaker, Kempler was not interested in theory, but rather helped people expand awareness, take responsibility for their actions, and gain a sense of authenticity and autonomy. (The latter would be difficult for caregivers.) See W. Kempler, *Experiential Psychotherapy with Families* (New York: Brunner/Mazel, 1981). Again like Whitaker, Kempler believed the family was key to individual maturity: H. Goldenberg and I. Goldenberg, *Family Therapy: An Overview*, 7th ed. (Belmont, CA: Thomson Brooks/Cole, 2008). (Perhaps that depends on one's definition of family, an idea that these pioneers had not yet considered. In my cotherapy with Carl Whitaker and thus direct observation, I saw that he gave primary emphasis to relationships and process, not simply to family structure.)

8. J. Cassidy, "Mind Games," *New Yorker*, September 18, 2006, 30–37.

9. A. P. Turnbull, J. M. Patterson, S. Behr, D. L. Murphy, J. G. Marquis, and M. J. Blue-Banning, eds., *Cognitive Coping, Families, and Disability* (Baltimore, MD: Brookes, 1993); in that volume, see P. Boss, "Boundary Ambiguity: A Block to Cognitive Coping," 257–270.

10. Perls, *Gestalt Therapy Verbatim*, 4.

11. The ongoing sadness of caregivers of adults with dementia may be similar to chronic sorrow, a term traditionally used to describe the long-term reactions of parents who have a child with a disability. See S. Olshansky, "Chronic Sorrow: A Response to Having a Mentally Defective Child," *Social Casework* 43 (1962): 190–193; and S. Roos, *Chronic Sorrow: A Living Loss* (New York: Brunner-Routledge, 2002).

12. For a full discussion of mourning in different cultures, see M. McGoldrick, J. M. Schlesinger, E. Lee, P. M. Hines, J. Chan, R. Almeida, B. Petkov, N. G. Preto, and S. Petry, "Mourning in Different Cultures," in *Living Beyond Loss: Death in the Family*, 2nd ed., ed. F. Walsh and M. McGoldrick (New York: Norton, 2004), 119–160.

13. P. Dilworth-Anderson and S. Marshall, "Social Support in Its Cultural Context," in *Handbook of Social Support and the Family*, ed. G. R. Pierce, B. R. Sarason, and I. G. Sarason (New York: Plenum, 1996), 61–79; *Roots*, DVD, directed by

D. Greene, G. Moses, J. Erman, and M. Chomsky (1977; Burbank, CA: Warner Home Video, 2002).

14. D. G. Faust, *The Republic of Suffering* (New York: Vintage, 2008).

15. Ibid.

16. Kenneth Gergen, a professor at Swarthmore College, said, "We all confront loss in our lives, and with loss comes a rupture in meaning." Quoted on book jacket of P. Boss, *Loss, Trauma, and Resilience* (New York: Norton, 2006).

17. S. Minuchin, *Families and Family Therapy* (Cambridge, MA: Harvard University Press, 1974).

18. E. Lindemann, "Symptomatology and Management of Acute Grief," *Journal of Psychiatry 101* (1944): 141–148.

19. D. S. Becvar, *In the Presence of Grief: Helping Family Members Resolve Death, Dying, and Bereavement Issues* (New York: Guilford Press, 2001); G. A. Bonanno, *The Other Side of Sadness* (New York: Basic, 2009); F. Walsh and M. McGoldrick, eds., *Living Beyond Loss: Death in the Family*, 2nd ed. (New York: Norton, 2004).

Chapter 5: The Psychological Family

1. E. Berscheid, "The Human's Greatest Strength: Other Humans," in *A Psychology of Human Strengths*,

ed. L. G. Aspinwall and U. M. Staudinger (Washington, DC: American Psychological Association, 2003), 42. See also E. Berscheid and H. T. Reis, "Attraction and Close Relationships," in *The Handbook of Social Psychology*, 4th ed., ed. D. T. Gilbert, S. T. Fiske, and G. Lindzey (New York: McGraw-Hill, 1998), 2:193–281.

2. Berscheid, "Human's Greatest Strength"; Berscheid and Reis, "Attraction and Close Relationships."

3. A psychological family is indeed a "mental representation of family, which may exist in addition to the family in which one actually lives": D. Becvar, review of *Loss, Trauma, and Resilience: Therapeutic Work with Ambiguous Loss*, by P. Boss, *Journal of Marital and Family Therapy* 32, no. 4 (October 2006): 531.

4. Berscheid, "Human's Greatest Strength"; M.E.P. Seligman, *Authentic Happiness: Using the New Positive Psychology to Realize Your Potential for Lasting Fulfillment* (New York: Free Press, 2002).

5. Berscheid, "Human's Greatest Strength," 41; H. T. Reis, W. A. Collins, and E. Berscheid, "The Relationship Context of Human Behavior and Development," *Psychological Bulletin 126* (2000): 844–872.

6. For the full story, see Boss, *Loss, Trauma, and Resilience*, 25, and P. Boss, *Ambiguous Loss* (Cambridge, MA: Harvard University Press, 1999), 1. In

1999, I wrote about the letters my father and his mother exchanged over the decades. Lives lived apart were still connected. I also wrote about them in an academic journal: P. Boss, "The Experience of Immigration for the Mother Left Behind: The Use of Qualitative Feminist Strategies to Analyze Letters from My Swiss Grandmother to My Father," *Marriage & Family Review 19*, nos. 3–4 (1993): 365–378. Reprinted in *Families on the Move: Migration, Immigration, Emigration, and Mobility*, ed. B. H. Settles, D. E. Hanks III, and M. B. Sussman (New York: Haworth, 1993), 365–378. In German (now translated), my Swiss grandmother, Sophie Salzmann Grossenbacher, wrote of her longing, too, for dear ones far away. Having read all of her letters, I understand that we had become her psychological family, just as she had become my father's; see Boss, *Ambiguous Loss*.

7. F. Russo, *They're Your Parents, Too!* (New York: Bantam, 2010).

8. P. Picasso, *The Tragedy*, 1903. Oil on wood, 41 $1/2$ × 27 $1/8$ in., Chester Dale Collection, National Gallery of Art, Washington, DC.

9. Berscheid, "Human's Greatest Strength," 41; Reis, Collins, and Berscheid, "Relationship Context of Human Behavior and Development."

10. K. Armstrong, *The Spiral Staircase* (New York: Knopf, 2004), 272.

11. Ibid., 298.

12. N. L. Paul, "The Use of Empathy in the Resolution of Grief," *Perspectives in Biology and Medicine 11* (1967): 153–169.

13. M. McGoldrick, R. Gerson, and S. Petry, *Genograms: Assessment and Intervention*, 3rd ed. (New York: Norton, 2008).

Chapter 6: Family Rituals, Celebrations, and Gatherings

1. S. J. Wolin and L. A. Bennett, "Family Rituals," *Family Process 23*, no. 3 (1984): 401–420.

2. B. H. Fiese, "Dimensions of Family Rituals Across Two Generations: Relation to Adolescent Identity," *Family Process 31* (1992): 151–162.

3. B. H. Fiese and C. A. Kline, "Development of the Family Ritual Questionnaire: Initial Reliability and Validation Studies," *Journal of Family Psychology 6*, no. 3 (1993): 290–299.

4. J.H.S. Bossard and E. S. Boll, *Ritual in Family Living: A Contemporary Study* (Philadelphia: University of Pennsylvania Press, 1950); L. A. Bennett,

S. J. Wolin, and K. J. McAvity, "Family Identity, Ritual, and Myth: A Cultural Perspective on Life Cycle Transitions," in *Family Transitions*, ed. C. Falicov (New York: Guilford Press, 1988), 211–234; E. Imber-Black and J. Roberts, *Rituals for Our Times* (New York: HarperCollins, 1992).

5. B. H. Fiese, K. A. Hooker, L. Kotary, and J. Schwagler, "Family Rituals in the Early Stages of Parenthood," *Journal of Marriage and Family 55* (August 1993): 634.

6. S. Dickstein, "Family Routines and Rituals—The Importance of Family Functioning: Comment on a Special Section," *Journal of Family Psychology 16* (2002): 441–444; S. R. Friedman and C. S. Weissbrod, "Attitudes Toward the Continuation of Family Rituals Among Emerging Adults," *Sex Roles 50*, nos. 3–4 (2004): 277–284.

7. M. McGoldrick, J. M. Schlesinger, E. Lee, P. M. Hines, J. Chan, R. Almeida, B. Petkov, N. C. Petro, and S. Petry, "Mourning in Different Cultures," in *Living Beyond Loss*, ed. F. Walsh and M. McGoldrick (New York: Norton, 2004), 119–160.

8. J. Roberts, "Setting the Frame: Definition, Functions, and Typology of Rituals," in *Rituals in Families and Family Therapy*, ed. E. Imber-Black, J. Roberts, and R. A. Whiting (New York: Norton, 2003), 3–48.

9. E. Imber-Black, "Rituals and the Healing Process," in *Living Beyond Loss*, ed. F. Walsh and M. McGoldrick (New York: Norton, 2004), 340–357.

10. Ibid.

11. Rituals also serve to fix who is in or out of your family (boundaries) and who does what (roles). According to sociologist Erving Goffman, rituals clarify and fix these roles and boundaries and thus stabilize the family. What to do, where to sit, how to act, when to speak—all are spelled out in a family's rituals that deal with birth and death, marriage and divorce, and ceremonies of transition to adulthood. See E. Goffman, *Interaction Ritual* (New York: Pantheon, 1967).

12. Imber-Black, "Rituals and the Healing Process."

13. I. Böszörményi-Nagy and G. Spark, *Invisible Loyalties* (New York: Harper and Row, 1973), 75.

14. Imber-Black, "Rituals and the Healing Process."

15. R. A. Whiting, "Guidelines to Designing Therapeutic Rituals," in *Rituals in Families and Family Therapy*, ed. E. Imber-Black, J. Roberts, and R. A. Whiting (New York: Norton, 1988), 84–112.

16. C. Geertz, *The Interpretation of Cultures* (New York: Basic, 1973), cited in M. W. deVries, "Trauma in Cultural Perspective," in *Traumatic Stress*, ed.

B. van der Kolk, A. C. MacFarlane, and L. Weisaeth
(New York: Guilford Press, 2007), 398–413.

17. Geertz, *The Interpretation of Cultures*, cited in
    deVries, "Trauma in Cultural Perspective," 402.

18. J. M. Beaton, J. E. Norris, and M. W. Pratt,
    "Unresolved Issues in Adult Children's Marital
    Relationships Involving Intergenerational
    Problems," *Family Relations 52*, no. 2 (2003):
    143–153.

19. F. Russo, *They're Your Parents, Too!* (New York:
    Bantam, 2010).

20. Wolin and Bennett, "Family Rituals"; Fiese and
    Kline, "Development of the Family Ritual Ques-
    tionnaire."

Chapter 7: Seven Guidelines for the Journey

1. A. B. Cohen, "Many Forms of Culture," *American
   Psychologist 64*, no. 3 (April 2009): 194–204.

2. H. Lavretsky, "Stress and Depression in Informal
   Family Caregivers of Patients with Alzheimer's Disease," *Aging Health 1*, no. 1 (August 2005): 117–133.

3. For this reason, we are now looking at caregiving
   through a stress process lens. See Lavretsky, "Stress
   and Depression."

4. Lavretsky, "Stress and Depression." See also W. Caron, P. Boss, and J. Mortimer, "Family Boundary Ambiguity Predicts Alzheimer's Outcomes," *Psychiatry: Interpersonal & Biological Processes 62*, no. 4 (1999): 347–356.

5. C. Buckley, *Losing Mum and Pup* (New York: Grand Central Publishing, 2009), 91; see also C. Goldman, *The Gifts of Caregiving* (Minneapolis, MN: Fairview Press in cooperation with the Center for Spirituality and Healing, University of Minnesota, 2002).

6. G. A. Bonanno, *The Other Side of Sadness* (New York: Basic, 2009).

7. H. Kushner, *When Bad Things Happen to Good People* (New York: Anchor, 2004).

8. This version of the Serenity Prayer is from E. Sifton, *The Serenity Prayer: Faith and Politics in Times of Peace and War* (New York: Norton, 2003), 7.

9. P. Boss, *Loss, Trauma, and Resilience* (New York: Norton, 2006), 177.

10. I use the term *attachment* in this section in a general sense. See J. Bowlby, *Attachment and Loss*, vol. 3, *Loss: Sadness and Depression* (New York: Basic Books, 1980).

11. T. Bowman, *Finding Hope When Dreams Have Shattered* (St. Paul, MN: Bowman, 2001).

12. B. Pym, *Excellent Women* (New York: Penguin, 1952), 11.

13. Lavretsky, "Stress and Depression."

Chapter 8: Delicious Ambiguity

1. The term *delicious ambiguity* was coined by therapist Joanna Bull of the Wellness Center, Santa Monica, California. See G. Radner, *It's Always Something* (New York: Simon & Schuster, 1989), 195.

2. Radner, *It's Always Something*, 268.

3. K. Tippett, host and producer, "Alzheimer's, Memory and Being," *On Being*, American Public Media, April 22, 2010. Transcript available at http://being.publicradio.org/programs/2010/alzheimers/transcript.shtml.

4. B. Howard, "The Secrets of Resilient People," *AARP*, November-December 2009, 32, 34–35.

5. L. S. Brady, "No Tethering, and It's All Good," *New York Times*, September 26, 2010, 17.

6. AARP, "How Resilient Are You?" *AARP*, November-December 2009, 34. Adapted from A. Seibert, *The Resiliency Advantage* (San Francisco: Berrett-Koehler, 2005).

7. C. Connolly, "Leaving," *All This and More: New and Selected Poems* (Minneapolis, MN: Nodin, 2009), 40.

Also see C. Connolly, *Payments Due* (St. Paul, MN: Midwest Villages & Voices, 1995).

8.   P. Hampl, *The Florist's Daughter* (Orlando, FL: Harcourt, 2007), 213–214.

9.   Hampl, *Florist's Daughter*, 211.

10. C. Stangl, *Third Play Guide* (Minneapolis, MN: Guthrie Theater, February 16–March 30, 2008).

11. J. P. Shanley, "Preface," *Doubt: A Parable* (New York: Dramatists Play Service, 2005), ix–x.

12. Elsewhere I have written in detail about spirituality in relation to ambiguous loss and why some people may be more tolerant of ambiguity than others. See P. Boss, *Loss, Trauma, and Resilience* (New York: Norton, 2006). Personality and upbringing matter. For our purposes here, however, know that you can learn to increase your tolerance for ambiguity. The goal is to manage complex situations that have no apparent solution. People with a spiritual worldview tend to be able to do this. They live life as it comes. Native Americans call it "harmony with nature." Also see P. Boss, *Ambiguous Loss: Learning to Live with Unresolved Grief* (Cambridge, MA: Harvard University Press, 1999).

13. M. S. Lane and K. Klenke, "The Ambiguity Tolerance Interface: A Modified Social Cognitive Model for Leading Under Uncertainty," *Journal*

of Leadership & Organizational Studies 10 (Winter 2004): doi:10.1177/107179190401000306.

14. J. D. Wigod, "Negative Capability and Wise Passiveness," *PMLA 67* (June 1952): 383–390.

15. M. H. Forman, ed., *The Letters of John Keats*, 2nd ed. (New York: Oxford University Press, 1935), 72.

16. I. D. Yalom, *Staring at the Sun* (San Francisco: Jossey-Bass, 2008, 2009).

17. Ibid., 5.

18. Ibid., 205.

19. Søren Kierkegaard is posthumously regarded as the father of existentialism. See G. Marino, "Søren Kierkegaard," in *Basic Writings of Existentialism* (New York: Modern Library, 2004), 7–106.

Chapter 9: The Good-Enough Relationship

1. P. Mishra, *An End to Suffering* (New York: Picador, 2004).

2. Most early family therapists agreed with Murray Bowen, not Whitaker. Bowen wrote about a "solid self" that would not participate in fusion. However, he and other theorists of the day (Salvador Minuchin, David Olson, Douglas Sprenkle, and Candyce Russell) did not consider the fused

attachments and unbalanced roles, when in older couples there may be dementia and caregiving. In such cases, a clear, solid sense of self is difficult to maintain, even for an emotionally healthy spouse. See M. Bowen, *Family Therapy in Clinical Practice* (New York: Aronson, 1978); S. Minuchin, *Families and Family Therapy* (Cambridge, MA: Harvard University Press, 1974); and D. H. Olson, D. H. Sprenkle, and C. Russell, "Circumplex Model of Marital and Family Systems: I. Cohesion and Adaptability Dimensions, Family Types, and Clinical Applications," *Family Process 18*, no. 1 (April 1979): 3–28.

3. N. Noddings, *Caring: A Feminine Approach to Ethics and Moral Education* (Berkeley: University of California Press, 1984); A. Maslow, "A Theory of Motivation," *Psychological Review 50*, no. 4 (1943): 370–396.

4. Noddings, *Caring*, 17–18.

5. K. Armstrong, *The Spiral Staircase* (New York: Knopf, 2004), 298.

6. P. Boss and L. Kaplan, "Ambiguous Loss and Ambivalence When a Parent Has Dementia," in *Intergenerational Ambivalences: New Perspectives on Parent-Child Relations in Later Life*, ed. K. Pillemer and K. Lüscher (Oxford, England: Elsevier, 2004), 207–224.

7. C. W. Sherman and P. Boss, "Spousal Dementia Caregiving in the Context of Late-Life Remarriage," *Dementia: The International Journal of Social Research and Practice 6* (May 2007): 245–270.

Conclusion

1. C. Goldman, *The Gifts of Caregiving* (Minneapolis, MN: Fairview Press in cooperation with the Center for Spirituality and Healing, University of Minnesota, 2002), 37.

2. E. Berscheid, "The Human's Greatest Strength: Other Humans," in *A Psychology of Human Strengths*, ed. L. G. Aspinwall and U. M. Staudinger (Washington, DC: American Psychological Association, 2003). See also E. Berscheid and H. T. Reis, "Attraction and Close Relationships," in *The Handbook of Social Psychology*, 4th ed., ed. D. T. Gilbert, S. T. Fiske, and G. Lindzey (New York: McGraw-Hill, 1998), 2:193–281.

A Note to Caregivers About Working with Health Care Professionals

1. P. Boss, *Loss, Trauma, and Resilience: Therapeutic Work with Ambiguous Loss* (New York: Norton, 2006).

2. See R.-J. Green and P. D. Werner, "Intrusiveness and Closeness-Caregiving: Rethinking the Concept of Family Enmeshment," *Family Process 35* (1996): 115–136.

3. V. Goldner, "Feminism and Family Therapy," *Family Process 24*, no. 1 (1985): 31–47.

4. Salvador Minuchin, a pioneer family therapist, calls it "enmeshment" and gave the following indicators of dysfunction: "interdependence of relationships, intrusion on personal boundaries, poorly differentiated perceptions of self and of other family members, and weak family subsystem boundaries," 1033. In S. Minuchin, L. Baker, B. L. Rosman, R. Liebman, L. Milman, and T. C. Todd, "A Conceptual Model of Psychosomatic Illness in Children," *Archives of General Psychiatry 32*, no. 8 (1975): 1031–1038. See also S. Minuchin, *Families and Family Therapy* (Cambridge, MA: Harvard University Press, 1974).

5. N. L. Mace and P. V. Rabins, *The 36-Hour Day* (Baltimore, MD: Johns Hopkins University Press, 2006).

6. American Psychiatric Association, *Diagnostic and Statistical Manual of Mental Disorders*, 4th ed., text revision (Washington, DC: American Psychiatric Association, 2000), 679–683, 736–737.

About the Author

Pauline Boss, PhD, is a groundbreaking scientist-practitioner who now shares her work with the general public. She is Professor Emeritus of Family Social Science at the University of Minnesota; a fellow in the American Psychological Association and the American Association of Marriage and Family Therapy; and former president of the National Council on Family Relations. She is also a family therapist in private practice in St. Paul, Minnesota. Dr. Boss coined the term *ambiguous loss* in the 1970s and summarized the research that led to her theory in the widely acclaimed book *Ambiguous Loss: Learning to Live with Unresolved Grief* (Harvard University Press, 1999). Her more recent book, *Loss, Trauma, and Resilience* (Norton, 2006), was written for professionals who work with families of the physically and psychologically missing. Although Dr. Boss is a lifelong Midwesterner, educated at the University of Wisconsin-Madison, she has since 1975 shared her work throughout the United States and around the world. She was a visiting professor at

215

Harvard Medical School (child psychiatry), University of
Southern California (gerontology), and Hunter School
of Social Work in New York City (Moses Professor).
Today Dr. Boss continues her clinical practice in St. Paul,
Minnesota. She also lectures and presents workshops
and keynote speeches, nationally and internationally. To
contact her, visit www.ambiguousloss.com.

Index